Divided You Fall

Creating an Appreciative Environment

J Robert Heinzman D.M.

March 4, 2016

Introduction

Now that you have opened the cover you are probably wondering what this book is about. Let me start by saying it is not about constitutions, common law, or uniting to overthrow governments. It is about each and every one of us on and off of the planet we call Earth.

It is about our past, our present, and possible futures. It is an exploration of understanding that we should put aside the past, we should learn our present strengths, and build the best possible positive future of us. Focus, or more correctly, past focus, present focus, and future focus is about reframing our perceptions.

Some of you reading this will feel uncomfortable and believe the focus is on history, religion, politics, culture, or business. The truth is it is about you, me, and everything around us.

I have broken the concepts into a discussion of manageable topics focusing on areas from history. The material is presented in a manner to reframe common perception issues that cause division. Understanding how perception makes us feel, and learning to rethink about situations promotes positive adjustment in our perceptions and helps us to overcome anti separatism. When we focus on the negative of a situation, person, or event division occurs and in the process we give up our empowerment to others rhetoric.

I believe each individual has an impact, and that each individual has a strength that contributes to the whole. Individuals get lost in the creation of teams, teams get lost in organizations. The loss occurs by focusing on a culture and a belief that teams are one and each person on the team should think and act the same. Cultural normative beliefs cause organizations to implement wide sweeping changes across organizations, departments, regions expecting everyone to accomplish the same level of performance.

Diversity is challenged due to cultural norms which can be a barrier to innovation and creativity. If we expect all individuals to work in the same manner within extremely narrow defined parameters, then we cannot expect individuals to think for themselves. The very nature of team takes away identity and attempts to indoctrinate an individual to move from an old state of being to a new *'preferred'* state which meets the company's definition of right.

Based on my research I believe there is an *'I'* in team. Individuals (*'I'*) matter and each of us brings a unique background, focus, and idea which helps to improve the whole.

As Plato alludes to in Book 1 of Laws, conflict begins with the individual. We must first overcome our own insecurity, balance of our selves must be obtained, learning who we are. An organization is made up of departments, those departments are made up of teams, and teams are made up of individuals. Each individual is unique and provides value in their unique abilities.

As you read I ask that you keep the following ideas in mind; problems are past, future is where possibilities lie, build on present strengths to build a positive future.

Together we can build an Appreciative Environment (AE). Let's explore how.

Table of Contents

In the Beginning..1

History is Important Isn't It?.......................................6

Christopher Columbus..7

Columbus the Tyrant – Past Focus..............................7

Columbus the Visionary – Present Focus...................13

Columbus's Legacy of Exploration – Future Focus......17

Thomas Edison...19

Edison the Bully – Past Focus....................................19

Edison the Entrepreneur – Present Focus..................23

Edison's Innovative Spirit – Future Focus..................27

Politics & Law, the great equalizer?..........................30

Royal Caribbean...31

Royal Caribbean exploits Haiti – Past Focus............31

Royal Caribbean Supports Haiti – Present Focus......32

Royal Caribbean lesson on Ethics – Future Focus......34

Retail Industry..35

Retail Slavery – Past Focus.......................................35

Retail Provides needed Jobs – Present Focus............37

Retail and Moral Opportunity – Future Focus...........40

WWII & Harry S. Truman..42

Truman drops a bomb – Past Focus............................42

Truman Saves Lives – Present Focus..........................44

Truman and the Cold War – Future Focus..................46

Morals and Ethics – Perception..................................48

Religion, are we really going there?..........................56

Religion - Past Focus..57

Religion - Present Focus...60

Religion - Future Focus..63

Where are we?...65

Quotes that Matter ~ Thinking Moments...................70

The Appreciative Environment..78

Business Application...78

Frederick Winslow Taylor...82

Taylor the Tyrant -Past Focus..82

Taylor the Thoughtful - Present Focus............................85

Taylor & Scientific Management – Future Focus.............91

George Elton Mayo..94

Mayo in the Dark – Past Focus......................................94

Elton Mayo on Target – Present Focus...........................96

Elton Mayo the Light – Future Focus.............................98

Management Theory continued.....................................101

Multiple Intelligences...107

Why should we care about AE?.....................................113

Leadership..123

Knowledge..133

Leaders affect on Followers Job Satisfaction...................136

The Model...137

Applying Appreciative Environment..............................142

Transparency...147

References...- 1 -

In the Beginning

In the beginning humans banded together in a family unit, or clans, and roamed an expanse of area taking up a couple acres per person to sustain the group. Each individual had a purpose to the sustainability of the clan. In these tight knit groups, the strongest was looked to as the leader, this leadership was a natural selection based on need.

Now my focus here is not about right and wrong, it is not about what place any person should be in, it is only a discussion of the relation between the society and the individual.

With our focus on early pre-civilization we can imagine the rule of 'law' is not about right or wrong it is about survival. In the pre-civilization when clanship was in the hunter gatherer stage if an individual wanted something they took it if they could. This survival of the fittest was needed to further the species.

Although, we can imagine that if an individual was really good at hunting strategy, and another individual wanted that person's belongings others might resist as a group.

Certain needs of the whole were still important, if only due to safety in numbers, and of course the need to eat.

At some point we came to realize that seeds grow, and when planted and taken care of crops grew. Other specialized needs in the division of labor came about. With this also came the need to band together with other clans to mate, till, and continuation. How does this burgeoning society keep a sense of order?

Therein lays the paradox, who will lead, what is the division of labor, how will we keep order within the society? Individual's rights become less due to laws, no longer can the strongest just take what is not theirs. As civilization's first businesses grow; farming, hunting, weaving, and politics, we begin to see hierarchy enter the picture. A cast system of those who rule and those who follow.

Individual rights, freedom, thoughts, begin to subside to the needs of society. Years before ideas like group think, brainstorming, and motivation, management ideals were more on division of labor to create high performance.

Management ideals were akin to the belief of specialization and that individual's rise to their place in society. Society had only become more complex and in society individuality was not appreciated.

Culture has been created by this ancient progress of creating a civilization, each with its ideas of right and wrong, good and bad, and a focus on what can you do for society. Individuality and diversity is hindered by culture. Culture by its very nature is a barrier to diversity and individuality. Management methods and the caste system placed everyone into a position.

Let's take a leap to the last hundred years and we see that things continue based on this historical cultural ideal and the individual.

During the early 1900's it was common that an individual joined a company and retired with that same organization.

During tenure with the organization those individuals found security, affirmation, and were committed to the organization.

During the baby boom generation, we saw work attitudes change from long term commitment to an organization, to a commitment to the organization only as long as I am valued.

In 2000 work attitudes took another transformative turn and began focusing on what's in it for me. The company focus of teaming, filtered out the individual. The problem with teaming is it does not naturally support diversity and individual initiative. We find individuals morphing their own cultural selves, and often their values, to become part of the group and in doing so losing their identity.

The change of self is extrinsic, cultural differences between the individual and the company only work as long as the individual values the relationship, this opens the opportunity for motivation and job satisfaction levels to drop. Groupthink, poor brainstorming, dis-satisfaction become prevalent due to the clash of ideals.

All of this difference has created a workforce of divided individuals all looking out for themselves and ignoring the team, department, and organization as a whole. It is in this disparity the individual has been lost to the socialization of society and corporations.

Scientific management proposed in 1911 that authority is based in knowledge not in position, by this same token a number of studies since have shown leadership can come from anywhere depending on the situation.

I bring up this idea to help us understand why we believe, what we believe, and to ask you to allow yourself to think outside the box you have been placed in by cultural perceptions.

How do we overcome the nature of things and eons of cultural focus? How do we embrace individuality to better the whole? What can we do to create an Appreciative Environment?

History is Important Isn't It?

To understand opportunities for building on strengths it is important to review how others may have missed opportunity and our perceptions. Certainly it is easy to poke at history but as we review don't get caught up in what occurred. It is more important to review these opportunities that were missed to understand possible strengths we may be missing today.

Removing barriers to creativity and innovation cannot occur if we are blind to others strengths. We will take a journey through Past focus (negatives), Present focus (strengths), and Future Focus (positives) and possibilities by reviewing a couple well-known historical figures. We will review the individual and circumstances, each viewpoint will lead us on a journey of thought and feelings.

Christopher Columbus

Columbus the Tyrant – Past Focus

Most of us have heard how in 1492 Christopher Columbus set out from Spain to find a new trade route to Asia and subsequently discovered America. Of course, we know now, he actually discovered the Bahamas off the South Eastern tip of Florida.

Christopher Columbus believed that he had discovered the West Indies, an assertion he carried till the day he died. When I say discovered, what Columbus did was open Europeans perception. His discovery proved yes there is land to the west, and his exploration showed there was value in going there.

Columbus was focused on an idea of finding the western route to Asia, this singular focus could not be diverted. The colony in Hispaniola became a base for finding gold and in his mind a jumping off point to Asia. Columbus believed the island to be off the coast of the Indies.

Yucatan Traders, and natives' knowledge of the area were ignored because of one idea, find the west passage to Asia.

He blindly believed his calculations of the distances and circumference of earth, which were incorrect. Columbus selectively used information to prove what he believed, selective perception, and ignored even his own countrymen. By the time Columbus made his fourth and last voyage, common knowledge among his countrymen was that the area was not Asia nor was it anywhere near Asia.

Today we know that Columbus did not discover America and we are not taught about his intolerance and narrow view of the world. How did his viewpoints evolve? In his early years he sailed the western coast of Europe and Africa north and south.

As a young man this period of time helped him learn to navigate and sail. It was during these early years traveling north that it is believed he heard of the land to the west. Due to his own calculations of the circumference of the world he believed the land to be Asia. Columbus's primary motive for traveling west was one of monetary greed.

Columbus as an individual had many flaws, and in hindsight we may state he had a lack of ethical and moral compass.

He ignored others and had a strong will in his own belief system. Columbus charisma and the Spanish Crowns hope of refilling the royal coffers was an opportunity of timing.

Thirty-three days after leaving the Canary Islands, off the coast of Africa, the crew began to see branches and flocks of birds. Sailors know this to be signs of land. The crew was promised that the first man to sight land was to receive a yearly pension of 10,000 maravedis for life (Roughly 120K – 140K in 2016 US dollars). On the morning of October 12 1492, a sailor named Rodrigo saw the light shining off the white sand beaches and cried out land. Later Columbus claimed he had seen the light the evening before and thus he claimed and received the reward.

Upon approaching the islands, the indigenous people (Arawaks) greeted the ships and sailors as they landed. They traded goods for beads and trinkets. Of course Columbus found the gold earrings and trinkets the natives wore of great interest.

Columbus sums up his thoughts in his journal. "They brought us parrots and balls and spears and many other things, which they exchanged for the glass beads and hawks' bells. They willingly traded everything they owned… They do not bear arms, and do not know them, for I showed them a sword, they took it by the edge and cut themselves out of ignorance. They would make fine servants… With fifty men we could subjugate them all and make them do whatever we want."

Of course the thing wanted most by Columbus and the Spanish crown was gold. The gold trinkets wore by the natives led to the singular thought of where is the gold? Columbus reported back to the Court of Madrid that the natives were so naïve and so free with their possession that no one who has not witnessed them would believe it. Columbus portrayed the natives as little more than children. The belief was the native would provide anything, one only had to ask, they never say no.

Along with the boast of bringing back as much gold as the Crown could want and as many slaves, prompted Ferdinand and Isabella to provide seventeen ships on Columbus return voyage to Hispaniola.

What followed is the enslavement of the indigenous people, gathered up in pens and piled on boats to be shipped back to Spain as slaves. Columbus and his men forced all Arawak's fourteen and older to collect gold. The quota had to be met every three months, upon meeting the quota the individual would be provided a copper token to hang around their neck. Those caught without a copper token would have their hands cut off and bled to death.

During this time Columbus as governor we see his atrocities and harsh totalitarian methods brought against the Arawak and Spaniards. Christopher Columbus and his brothers kept much of the little wealth generated by the colony for themselves. The atrocities against the Spaniards and Columbus's poor administrative skills was the breaking point.

As the crisis peaked Columbus sent for assistance from Spain. The crown sent Francisco de Bobadilla as Governor, he soon identified Columbus as the problem and sent him and his brothers back to Spain in chains in 1500.

Christopher's early days as a trader and belief that Europeans and Christian's faith are superior caused him, as many at that time did, to believe his knowledge was greater than the indigenous peoples of South America. His poor governing skills caused his removal as governor of Hispaniola and subsequent time in prison due to his poor administrative abilities.

After his arrest he later convinced the crown to support one more voyage, the fourth, were he wound up stranded with 200 men on Jamaica for a year. One of his greatest failures was his inability to see what was right before him, the New World. Columbus never accepted that he had not found Asia, even when the rest of Europe was convinced America was a previously unknown territory.

Columbus the Visionary – Present Focus

It is easy to poke holes in Columbus because we are separated by time and different cultural realities. Today we know that what occurred was a clash of cultures and a different perspective of value and ownership. We know if Columbus had not traveled to the new world, within fifty years' technology in ship building would have made the voyages inevitable. Looking at Columbus in a Past only focus makes it very difficult to see any strengths. The baggage of the past focus makes it easy to point fingers and think poorly of Columbus.

We forget that at the time, 1400's, Columbus's belief system was typical of his culture. We may forget that often great visionaries are of singular purpose and without training those skills cannot be transferred to other endeavors. Columbus was a sailor, navigator, and adventurer, he was not a scholar, politician, or negotiator. He took people's word as binding and guided his actions through blinding religious faith. Let's look at the individual and the strengths of the man through present focus.

Columbus had a vision, in having a vision he focused on how to accomplish the objective. His superior sailing skills, learned from years of sailing, his map making skills, and use of navigation techniques were key in achieving the vision. His vision required going outside the norm and to challenge conventional wisdom. Similar to effective leaders who thoroughly understand their industry, Columbus business was sailing and navigating, which he excelled at.

He was willing to take risks. At a time when it was dangerous to sail past the Canary Islands Columbus believed he could navigate the unchartered waters. He put his life and reputation on the line to achieve what he believed was a calculated risk of making the west passage to Asia.

He was persistent and resilient, even after being turned down by England, France, and Portugal Columbus did not give up on his idea and eventually persuaded King Ferdinand and Queen Isabella of Spain to support his venture. He created the marketing pitch and refined it until he was able to persuade the right person at the right time.

Ultimately the west passage to Asia was not to be found, although Columbus was flexible and adaptable. He could have returned empty handed or sailed on, instead he realized the opportunity of the discovery and turned failure into success. The New World opened up wealth and opportunities for Spain which helped propel it forward as a super power of the time. On returning to Spain after the first voyage Columbus was able to salvage the experience and turn it into success.

In order to make the journey across the expanse of unknown unchartered waters Columbus had to be a leader. It had to be a combination of situational leadership being forceful, inspirational, charismatic, visionary, and belief in the crew and his own abilities. When faced with challenges he had to stand tall and lead his crew to success, he had to motivate them to achieve and overcome obstacles.

Columbus overcame his upbringing which would have him be a wool weaver and cheese merchant. He went to sea between ten and fifteen years of age.

He sailed on trading and slaving vessels. He was a very religious person who believe God was behind all opportunities. While sailing he learned much about navigating and map making. His ability as a sailor was second to none. His religious beliefs and sailing ability made him confident to take on the challenges of the time. The acts which occurred after discovering the New World was a cultural collision. If Columbus had not landed during this time, within Fifty years' others from Europe would have.

By focusing on the past and looking at the errors we spend our time counterproductively debating the mistakes that were made. Focusing on present strengths we see the real challenge that was overcome. Through viewing strengths, the opportunities to the future are open. We begin to appreciate the individual for their focus and look to future possibilities.

Columbus's Legacy of Exploration – Future Focus

Columbus voyage helped open European views toward the west and the opportunities the new land provided. In this New World there was untapped value which would allow unprecedented growth foe Europe. The dependency on Asia was diminished and a new age of exploration occurred. Let's take a look at Columbus and Europe in a Present focus.

The traits which led Columbus to go west continued, it showed that one man could make a difference. The charm of Columbus is not in what he did wrong but in what he did. He proved that any man could rise in position through hard work and determination. His legacy of exploration lived on through the discovery of South West passage and North America. By the time the Puritans decided it was time to find a new home to practice their religious freedom the New World was open.

The Great Expansion westward in the United States was driven in the same spirit and entrepreneurialism. Columbus is a story of will power and how we can overcome obstacles.

The individual can make a difference, it is up to each individual to make a moral, ethical, decision of what they want to be. As a world we have moved out of the dark ages, moved forward in technology, and provided more opportunities to create and innovate. We must be careful of dwelling on the past, lest we make the grave error of believing all possibilities have past us.

John F. Kennedy stated at the beginning of the space race that we will go to the moon not because it is easy but because it is hard. He believed that we could take the best of each of us and build a better future by overcoming obstacles. Today more opportunity is present for each of us because we know that hard work and determination, can lead to better futures. It is up to each of us to look for possible strengths in ourselves and each other to build a positive possible future.

Thomas Edison

Edison the Bully – Past Focus

Most of us know Thomas Edison and the story of how he discovered the light bulb. He was the creator of the phonograph, moving picture, and General Electric which started as Edison General Electric. Popular viewpoints state that of the 1093 patents filed in his name only one was probably an original idea. During Edison's life he did not actually invent he was an innovator.

An example of Edison's close mindedness occurs in 1884. Edison employed a young immigrant engineer to assist him in electric power generation. The young engineer, Nikola Tesla, felt higher voltage Alternating Current (AC) was a better direction to go. Edison believed AC – powered motors were too dangerous and insisted he focus on Direct Power DC. Edison promised Tesla $50,000, as a bonus, if he could improve the DC generators, called Dynamos at the time. After working on the Dynamo for several months Tesla made significant advances and improved the Dynamo.

When Tesla requested his reward, Edison told him that when he became a full-fledged American he would learn to appreciate an American joke.

Tesla left the employment of Edison and continued his work on AC power. Tesla teamed with George Westinghouse to bring the idea of electric power to the public. Throughout this period of time Edison continued to bully Tesla and undermine AC power advances. Edison was ideologically and financially invested in DC power. Edison embarked on a smear campaign through media and using high voltage AC power to electrocute animals, stray dogs, cats, cattle, horses, and Topsy the elephant.

Edison used his influence to encourage authorities, looking for an alternative method to execute death row inmates, to use AC power as the new source. When asked whether electrocution was a humane method of execution, Edison claimed that with Westinghouse's AC power it was humane.

Edison hoped to prove how dangerous AC power was and was willing to bend ethics and morals to bend perception to meet his needs.

The first electrocution was not humane; it took eight minutes overall to end the torture of the inmate. The man literally burned to death from the inside out.

Edison has been reported as a thief in some circles, and as proof the incandescent light bulb is provided. In 1878 Joseph Swan demonstrated the electric lamp to the Newcastle Chemical Society in England. Swan was not the first, he used Humphry Davy's battery, two wires, and a charcoal strip design from 1809. The strip glowed, making it the first electric lamp.

Warren De la Rue enclosed a platinum coil in an evacuated tube around 1819 to create the incandescent bulb. Edison reportedly saw Swan's demonstration in 1879, the demonstration also noted the shortcomings of the lamp. The lamp only burned 40 hours, in order to be viable it would need to burn longer. Edison realized the deficiency in the design, although Swan held the patent and the upper hand so we would think.

Swan was not dynamic in his marketing nor did he have the backing needed to further research the filament. Edison, who at this time was successful and had the monetary means merged Edison Electric with Swan Electric Light. Edison put Swan to work and eventually took all credit for the discovery through his name brand.

Edison was an opportunist, underhanded, and willing to go to extreme measures to protect his interests. He was singular of focus when he believed that he was right. His shortsightedness cost him the chance to control power generation. Edison power and light became General Electric and was controlled by JP Morgan.

Edison the Entrepreneur – Present Focus

Looking back at what Thomas Edison accomplished we need to look past the onus some in history have put on him and focus on the reality. Edison was a visionary and very gifted in physics, engineering, design, and marketing. Marketing and innovation were his strongest attributes. There is a distinct difference between innovation and invention. Improvement of design is innovative, and when innovation occurs the individual who can market the newest contraption will most likely be successful. It is natural to focus on the individual and the company that made the innovation occur over those who invented the idea in the first place.

Edison's purpose of defaming Westinghouse and Tesla was in part his strong belief in how dangerous AC power was. He had firsthand knowledge of AC power base don his experiments. At this time his research lab had been working on developing the electric chair for the purpose of a 'humane' method to dispose of death row inmates.

His second motivation was of course the realization that AC power could take profits away from his business. Edison was involved with JP Morgan selling DC power locally for the purpose of electric lighting.

Edison came from a middle class household and had access to good education. He was unable to fit into regular school due to his unique way of looking at the world. Today we would probably identify his inquiry and disruptive behavior as attention deficit disorder. Due to the lack of appropriate accommodation at that time he was forced to be home schooled by his mother. Edison's mother was an educated woman, she not only could work with him on a personal level, and she was also able to provide proper schooling.

Due to Edison's interest in science he later required a tutor, his parents were not equipped to explain the scientific concepts adequately. He excelled at physics, math, engineering and technology overall. He had the ability to see how something worked and envision methods to make them better.

It is there in his unique technical mind and ability to see how things work, and methods to improve them, that Edison excelled. His innovative spirit and entrepreneurialism made him the right person at the right time in history to help propel technology forward. He did not invent AC power although later he did improve the distribution process and make it possible to provide affordable power to the populace.

He had an innate ability to see ability in others and support those abilities to innovate new products. One story of Edison and his ability to motivate comes during the effort to improve the light bulb.

One of Edison's lab technicians working on the project is nervous and seems to be avoiding Edison. Edison confronts the technician and asks what is wrong. The technician tentatively explains he has failed a thousand experiments in the effort to improve the light bulb. Edison sternly tells the lab technician that he has not failed, he has only proven a thousand ways it will not work.

Edison had a unique ability to focus and see possibilities and capitalize on them. When others were unable to see potential he often found it. In his time, he was considered an inventor and a rock star of the industrial revolution. During this period of time invention and innovation were synonymous. Edison is the definition of what an entrepreneur is. He understood how technology works, he knew how to find ways to use it, he improved technology so it was useful, and he knew how to market his ideas.

Edison's Innovative Spirit – Future Focus

Early on Edison invented the electronic polling machine, it was his first, and some say, only true invention. There was no market for the machine because politicians felt it would give the majority a voice over the minority. This experience with the voting machine caused Edison to vow never to invent something others did not want or need.

Through thoughtful endeavor he understood what the public wanted and capitalized on it to build one of the most powerful companies in the world, General Electric, providing 100,000's of jobs. Even if he felt slated by the name change, he was the catalyst and continues to be the innovative spirit behind GE as stated on their about us web page.

Edison's actions provide insight into the steps of innovation and debunking of myths. Innovation does not occur in a vacuum. Innovation does not occur by chance or accident. Innovation happens in steps a little at a time and requires investment in time and resources.

To achieve innovation, we know that it requires hard work in a specific direction. This is akin to Edison's early lessons of building something no one wants. Innovation requires a change in direction. Doing the same thing over and over and getting the same results is not progress. Innovators see what is and isn't working, and realize the change that is needed. Innovation requires curiosity and experimentation.

Edison showed the importance of this when he recognized failure was part of the process, and was able to recognize the lab technician had not failed but proven 1000 ways something wouldn't work.

Innovation requires monetary support. Edison knew he needed to sell the products and focused on opportunities where the public's wants and needs could be met. Innovation grows from a desire to fit a need to accomplish a broader goal. Edison was able to see the potential of the light bulb but knew it needed to be improved to be a viable product.

Entrepreneurs thrive on discovery and vision. The ability to see what others cannot and then to work toward the successful creation of that vision is part of Edison's legacy. His can do spirit is behind many industrial products, transportation, power transmission, and medical equipment.

What strengths can you build on today that will lead to the next great opportunity or innovation? Do not let the minds in the box tell you it can't be done or that it has already been done. There is room for improvement and it only takes focus on the future possibilities.

Politics & Law, the great equalizer?

Plato discusses in Book Nine of Laws that laws are inherently written for good men, to guide them in how to interact with one another in socialized society. Laws are also for the sake those who left to their own volition would otherwise possibly do harm.

Legislators Legislate out of necessity, in the hope that there is no need for their laws. Laws are not equal in Plato's day, laws are administered to freemen and slave, to poor and rich, but each has a different level and each is treated based on the culture they are in. Law is akin to an ethical and moral issue of the perceived right and wrong. Let's explore this by reviewing business and corporate governance.

Royal Caribbean

Royal Caribbean exploits Haiti – Past Focus

In 2010 Haiti was devastated by a 7.0 earthquake. In the aftermath I recall news media online, TV, and print reporting that Royal Caribbean International was still berthing ships on a five-acre peninsula leased from the Haitian government. Many patrons were distraught and sick over the idea of enjoying themselves on the beach while in Port-au-Prince tens of thousands of people were dead and survivors were starving and looking for food and water. Cruise critics took to the internet, the news media reported the extravagance and ongoing exploitation of Haiti. The act of taking tourists to Haiti in the aftermath was looked at as a sickening act of greed. Many questioned how, during a time when thousands are suffering, how can an individual or a company justify such actions? When we view this from an ethical right and wrong it is easy to feel for the Haitian peoples and believe the cruise companies were acting in self-interest.

Royal Caribbean Supports Haiti – Present Focus

Let's look into the cruise and retail industry a little further. As stated earlier it is easy to find fault in the actions when faced with such atrocities occurring by nature or culture to the Haitian and third world populations. Government politics is not the same in all regions, laws are not identical, and what is right in one culture may be wrong in another.

Business is about making a profit. If a business does not continue to gain profit, jobs will be lost, tax dollars will not be available, and the end result is economic hardship. When business is taken away from an area, dollars cannot be spent and thus economic hardship can occur. The period of time after the 2010 earthquake in Haiti, cruise ships provided economic stability to that region. Tourism made up approximately 60 – 70% of the economy in Haiti.

The decision to continue to utilize Labadee beach, which was close to the epicenter of the earthquake, came after considerable debate within the Royal Caribbean Cruise Line.

According to the UN special envoy, Leslie Voltaire, Labadee was critical to Haiti's recovery; hundreds of people in Haiti rely on Labadee for their livelihood. I recall during the period after the earthquake that cruise ships were also carrying much needed supplies and personnel to Haiti. The company felt that ethically and morally they could not abandon the Haitian populace when Haiti needed help the most.

Royal Caribbean could have gone to any of its other ports and closed the Labadee port during this time of crisis, although it felt the monetary influx to the region would continue to help the island pull out faster. On many levels this is the responsible thing for a company to do. When making an investment in a community it seems only right that a company become vested in the local area. This investment should not only be present during good times, but bad as well.

Royal Caribbean lesson on Ethics – Future Focus

Royal Caribbean used Food for the Poor to distribute supplies, rice, beans, powdered milk, water, and canned foods. The company spent $55 million updating Labadee. The company employs hundreds on Labadee and hundreds more benefit from the market. 50% of the global workforce is employed in a service industry, 34% are in some type of production, and only 6% are employed in agriculture. With service industry employment being so high, it sheds light on why it was so important for Royal Caribbean to continue operations.

Retail Industry

Retail Slavery – Past Focus

Let's look at another industry which is infamous for making money off the backs of poor people in second and third world countries. The mass market clothing manufacturing industry, where the conditions of the laborers, at the fabrication level cause the term sweatshop to be used repeatedly. The term 'sweatshop' is identified as having two or more labor violations. Violations such as hazardous working conditions, poor wages under $38 us dollars a month, in areas like Bangladesh, and over 12-hour work shifts. Children under the age of fourteen, who are blocked from education, are working in these shops. The conditions are deadly in many ways, including laborers dying from exhaustion from long hours, illness, and beatings due to poor quality of work.

The only goal we can glean from these shops is one of greed. According Protests American companies utilizing these sweatshops to produce products are corrupt and should be ashamed.

The reality of these shops is akin to slavery through indentured servitude, and many cases of outright slavery in some areas of the world. The previous discussion is certainly grievous on many levels and it is easy for us to find fault. Human nature drives us to feel for these individuals.

Further review of corporate governance and actions taken by companies can lead us to believe greed is the only driver. Company's benevolence may be where the capital and cash flow take them.

Retail Provides Needed Jobs – Present Focus

A harder subject to find positive strength in is the retail trade industry and the numerous human rights violations which have occurred due to utilizing low cost laborer, indentured servitude, and in some cases out right slavery. Out of retail there have been some positives such as providing opportunities through cottage industry. The money spent to pay laborers provides jobs were none may have been before.

Over time, with ethical and moral support from companies, the industry can bring much needed jobs which are fair and non-exploitive. When corporations enter into business in those underserved countries, global awareness has heightened on the conditions of those areas.

Without the low cost labor, many developed economic countries would not be able to live the quality of life they are accustomed to.

Anyone who has a child knows that a pair of shoes are usually worn out in six months, the cost and quality of the shoe doesn't matter, kids know how to wear out shoes, or they outgrow them.

Without Wal-Mart, Costco, Target, and other low cost distributors vying for low cost manufactured goods, the cost to clothe our children would be prohibitive. Certainly the use of second hand stores would become more prevalent, although those not in the 1% would have socially outcast children.

In the new millennium we have seen many industries move toward fair trade systems. Due to watch dog organizations, and the fair trade systems, we are seeing companies doing a better job (certainly more can be done) of policing those contract manufacturers who produce product for them. As with Royal Caribbean, the investment in those areas should focus on ethical and moral treatment of workers, fair wages for the area, and human rights.

It is not my intent to say the working conditions in third world countries is a reason to celebrate.

The reality is that economic drivers depend on being able to produce products at a low enough cost that a profit can be maintained to continue the economy globally. Certainly a perfect system does not exist today, although we can improve through focusing on opportunities and not ignoring need.

Retail and Moral Opportunity – Future Focus

When we focus on the negative we do not allow ourselves to embrace the fact that the global economy in developed and developing countries has continued to rise.

Income levels are higher today with 79% of working individuals in 2010 making an income higher than the poor income index level as measured by the UN Global Economist. That means 79% make at least $1.25 U.S. Dollars an hour.

According to global household income ratings $1.25 is a low to middle income for an average size family of three to four, depending on the region. Coincidentally in the United States, Canada, and other developed areas, this is considered poor. The fact that $1.25 an hour is considered poor in the U.S, Canada, and other developed countries, is a factor in our perception. I encourage you to review MSN or Yahoo Finance yourself, don't forget to check your exchange rates for the current day.

This is a beginning, and yes certainly more can and should be done. The point here is if we only view the negative we do not take the time to realize income into a region means opportunities for education, health care, basic needs of shelter, food, and clothing. When we spend more time complaining we focus less time on improving.

Developing nations encourage companies to use their labor forces. When developed countries use developing countries it causes us to focus on that region. The focus, whatever our perception of right and wrong, on those regions heightens and we take notice. It is not always what we would agree is ethical or moral, but we need to realize those areas need opportunities.

Corporations have an opportunity to invest in those regions in an ethical, moral, and responsible manner. We have an opportunity to look for ways to help improve others conditions when we are in a position to do so.

Complaining about a problem without posing a solution is whining ~ Theodore Roosevelt.

WWII & Harry S. Truman

Truman drops a bomb – Past Focus

In 1945 U.S. President Harry Truman made the decision to drop the Atomic bomb on Hiroshima and Nagasaki. The dropping of the two atomic bombs killed over a 100,000 people. The cost of the Manhattan Project is reported to have been two billion dollars. An inquiry by congress was being sought, and would have endangered Truman's re-election. Many in congress felt the dollars spent on the Atomic Bombs were misappropriated funds. Numerous revisionist point to this act as political, and little to do with ending the war and forcing Japan to surrender.

We can find discussions on the internet which point to Truman's goal as killing as many Japanese as possible. The focus at the time was that Japanese could not be treated as normal humans. The 'Japs' were little barbarians according to Truman, his Generals, and the general U.S. Population. The bomb was not dropped on a military base; it was dropped on the Japanese civilian population.

Dropping the bomb covered up any talk of misappropriations and kept the U.S. Congress from holding hearings, which could have kept Truman from obtaining another term in office. Re-election would have been impossible if the public learned of the money spent, and the weapon that could end the war had been shelved. The final motive was to prove to the world that the U.S. was willing to use weapons of mass destruction.

Ethics are not clear cut, there are a number of differing opinions on ethics from utilitarian, deontology, and absolution to name a few. It is important to realize that ethics is not cut and dry, morals and ethics are culturally driven and will differ in perception based on our belief systems. Learn from our past, focus on the present strength, and envision the possible positive future.

Truman Saves Lives – Present Focus

In 1945 Truman had a hard decision to make. Dropping the bomb on civilians is not what civilized countries do. At the time the projected U.S. casualty numbers for an invasion of mainland Japan were estimated by a joint war plans committee at 46,000 U.S. troops. The losses during the latter part of the war were three enemy to every one ally. According to the joint war plan committee's estimate the actual totals of 130,000 plus was not out of the question.

After the war the troop strength was found to be greatly-underestimated, the actual Japanese strength was 900,000 which is more than the 560,000 estimated by Admiral Leahy in August of 1945. Operation Olympic would have taken place in November of 1945, by that time the Japanese troop strength could have easily tripled. Also, in hindsight we now know soldiers were training civilian populations. Based on previous battles the U.S. knew the Japanese would die fighting and not surrender.

In Okinawa twice as many Japanese died as did U.S. soldiers. The real possibility is that two million soldiers, Japanese and U.S. could have died had the invasion occurred. Today we can look at the reasons the bomb was used and realize it was a combination of punishment, justification of cost, saving lives, and ending the war as quickly as possible. In the grand scheme, the use of the bomb saved lives.

If an invasion occurred the death toll would have been much higher and the war would have ended much later. The use of the atomic bomb at that time did have the effect of ending the war quickly and limiting loss of life. In this case we see the end justified the means for the greater good. This of course is a utilitarian view point.

Truman and the Cold War – Future Focus

Politics is a constant battle of balance between right and wrong. Compromise becomes a real moral dilemma when trying to weigh out the next best path. In my reflection of Truman and the decision to drop the bomb the results proved the U.S. was a world power. Winning WWII propelled the U.S. into a position as the leader of the free world and it came out of the war with Americans earning enough money to purchase goods and seek a better life.

Out of WWII the reality of diplomatic cooperation globally became more apparent. The U.S. had been more isolation focused before WWII, after the U.S. became a global leader. The world learned that the use of the bomb was possible, it also knew it didn't want to have a reason to use it again. I recall in 1985 a General over the Pershing II missile forces in Germany mention that knowing the devastation that occurred at Nagasaki and Hiroshima makes us think before pushing the launch button.

The atomic age is not perfect but it has brought new opportunities in transportation, communications, education, medicine, and global focus to name a few.

Morals and Ethics – Perception

This is a good point to discuss morals and ethical philosophy. Ethics is based on cultural views and driven by our perception of reality. Morals is our individual perception of right and wrong, and can be shaped by our ethics.

Utilitarianism doctrine believes the morally correct action is the one that brings the greatest good to the greatest number of people. The result of actions maximizes the total benefit without regard to the distribution of benefits and burdens.

Deontology tends to follow moral code in a manner of though shalt not kill and recognition of treating humanity well. Deontology maintains the wrong in an action intrinsic, rather than the consequences it brings about.

Moral absolution is a view which believes some actions are wrong no matter the consequences. Moral absolution differs from deontology by endorsing two claims: some actions are intrinsically right or wrong, and the consequences of this sort (e.g. profiting on others pain) can never override its intrinsic rightness or wrongness.

Ethics and morals perceived by one is not the same as perceived by another. There are overlaps in theory based on the situation one comes across. For example, an individual may believe that education is a pathway to success, while another may believe that having skills and ability are required for success. Some individual would envision education as a method to provide opportunity but success depends on ability and skill as well. This underlying premise of how we view the world and others is what causes conflict which is unreasonable.

Answer this question; is manipulation good or bad? I ask this question of my students before discussing conflict and negotiation to provide a framing for the discussion. Many of us see manipulation as someone trying to get us to do something against our will. What I ask you is if the outcome of the manipulation is to help you earn more money, based on the skills that come from the manipulation, is that good or bad. It is in this frame of mind that conflict should lie if possible. We need conflict and negotiation to debate the benefits and the opportunities of a given path.

We have conflict on a daily basis from which route to work one should take to should we buy lunch or take it with us, or maybe you skip lunch altogether. In my opinion skipping lunch would be a bad outcome although it is not necessarily evil. Innovation and entrepreneurship depend on conflict and negotiation, trial and error and learning from our mistakes for better outcomes. This is where research lies and discussion lives dynamically providing better futures. The examples previously are provided to give us an opportunity to view topics in a new context through critical thinking. Following is a short discussion on the research of engineering education in the early 1900's. Education has been an issue since before the time of Socrates, what the best teaching method is, what the best material to teach is, what constitutes an average knowledge versus superior knowledge.

Perception Case

In 1918 Charles Mann did research on Engineering Education for the purpose of understanding if engineering education programs across different universities was adequate. The research was funded by the Carnegie foundation with a concern to understand the growing field of engineering. The research focused on a number of interesting correlations between education and its impact on society. Depending on your view point will drive your perception of the good and bad of the education system at that time. My aim here is not to cover every detail nor is it to tell you what is good or bad.

At the time of the research was performed there was a concern the curriculum provided was not consistent, the cost of education was rising out of proportion, and a great number of students failed to gain satisfactory engineering knowledge which left graduates unable to deal with the practical problems presented in industry upon leaving engineering schools.

Mann presented to the foundation that the focus on the curriculum did not prepare students properly due to the focus of the course material. For example, math, which is the most important tool of an engineer, was taught over a two-year period in separate courses. Mann felt the separation of the math courses was a source of weakness and did not focus on the student's needs. Mann believed the courses of algebra, coordinate geometry, and calculus to be part of one subject of mathematics. Courses should utilize case studies and practical application to increase the aptitude and preparation of students for industry.

The focus on graduation showed that fifty percent (50%) of engineering students dropped during their freshman year. Faculty believed that the drop rate was justification of a properly rigorous curriculum. Industry studies showed that many of those dropped due to grades went on to be proficient engineers due to their ability and skill.

Many students dropped due to English and writing and no due to mathematics and engineering principles. This led to further conclusions that the curriculum was flawed and was not properly designed for engineering students.

In the last ten years a number of papers have been published discussing engineering education and the need to revamp the methods. The research within these papers points to a lack of real-world application in engineering design and operations. Engineering courses need to provide engineering curriculum in the first year focusing on multidisciplinary analysis, design, critical thinking, and soft skills. Teach material in a form that relates the theory to practical application and in context.

Within these studies an industry review was performed. Students who did not obtain a degree in 1914 often went on to be competent engineers. In recent years non-degreed individuals with talent have shown their acumen as competent engineers.

One of the concerns brought up in these studies was whether the curriculum was properly focused toward engineering degrees. In the early 1900's the concern was failure due to requiring too much English, history, and multiple math courses in the first two years. Recent studies point to management, business acumen, and leadership courses causing dropouts.

The studies performed by Mann in 1914 to 1918 and the recent articles up through 2016 also show that engineering education persists to focus on a non-case study method and may not produce the strongest engineering graduates. The methods of teaching may be flawed and still need addressed.

In this short discussion we see that little attention seems to have been given to the early studies. Our task here is to ask critically why the same thing is being done if the result is still the same. This review is short and as stated does not cover all aspects of the studies performed.

Critical thinking leads us to believe we have a plausible argument but do we have a valid argument. Is this where ethical dilemma begins, in our perceptions of truth. Could the truth of the matter be that the faculty is correct and curriculum should stay as is in order to weed out those who cannot cut academic rigor? Is the course curriculum and methods of teaching correct? Are good competent engineering candidates truly being weeded out?

This is only an example of types of scenarios and questions which cause conflict. It is up to each of us to look at situations and find the best course of action based on the validity of the argument. When addressing a conflict, the outcome will be positive if we remember each person comes to the table with a genuine belief in their perception.

Appreciate the opinion, this doesn't mean we agree, look at the strength of the present situation to find a plausible direction going forward. Sometimes the only strength is the fact someone is willing to listen and discuss their view.

Religion, are we really going there?

Let's a take a short journey and review the dark ages, suffrage, and war. The following discussion is not about who is right or wrong. Religion has had a place throughout society as a focal point of the culture.

The history of religion tells us that confusion of what is God and what does God want has caused, and still does, divisions, cruelty, and miscommunication. If one is part of a specific religion that is the predominant of the area then it brings people together in cultural harmony.

His Holiness the Dalai Lama states in his 2010 book, *Toward a True Kinship of Faiths,* "There is no need for temples; no need for complicated philosophy. Our own brain, our own heart is our temple; the philosophy is kindness."

It is not my purpose to point at any religion as good or bad, the focus here is what has occurred in the name of God, as defined by each individual religion.

Religion - Past Focus

In the past two thousand years starting with intolerance for difference of opinion on what is right in Gods eyes to today we see terror in the form of war, inquisitions, secular division, and murder. Those of Jewish faith, in the time of Jesus, had him crucified for heresy. Voicing your opinion and belief that we are all children of God was taboo.

According to *National Geographic and the History of World Religions* Islamic faith states Christian and Jewish states must be destroyed and their lands conquered. Shortly after the Prophet Muhammad's death in 632 A.D. the Muslim armies spread out and conquered Palestine, Syria, Egypt, North Africa, and Spain. Killing and conquering Christian strongholds of the old world became the method to spread the word of Islam.

Fearing the end of Christianity Pope Urban II called upon the knights of Christendom to push back the conquests of Islam. The act of the crusades in the name of God again caused wide spread bloodshed, rape, pillaging, and devastation.

In the mid 1400's Spain purged the Muslims and reinstated Christianity as the main religion. Under Christianity (Catholicism), and the name of God, the Inquisitor General Tomás Torquemada forced Jews and Muslims to convert or leave Spain. Through torture, rape, and murder those who stayed were forced to confess their heresy or die. Unfortunately, the penalty for heresy was death, although the death was swift instead of long and torturous.

Under many core religions such as Christianity, Judaism, Muslim, Hinduism, and Buddhism women were and are second class citizens with specific roles for the sexes. This inequality has continued to keep women oppressed and even today has an impact on their opportunities. Religion halted progress of science, tolerance, and has been used as an excuse to enslave individuals of so called inferior status. Europeans believed that the indigenous peoples of the new world were savages and soulless, thus deserved to be slaves.

Into the 20th century at a time when we have progressed so far in technology, healthcare, and science we still see religion holding back understanding and tolerance for differences.

The past is past; the future is for us to decide. Tolerance as discussed by His Holiness the Dalai Lama and achieving a kinship in faith should be an opportunity not a divider. Let's take a look at religion and the strength it has.

Religion - Present Focus

Certainly there is many items we could point at based on our own experiences, cultures, and opinions that cause us to question religious focus. Let's take a moment and look at the strength that religion has offered throughout the ages.

In Antiquity and through the Middle Ages, when most made a living working the land, it was difficult to get an education. Religion was an avenue to education in the form of reading, arithmetic, and writing. Those who could afford education in Europe turned to the Church for education. Church was the educational force because Monks needed to know how to read and write in order to copy and distribute manuscripts.

The perceived need to get the word out to the masses about religion was a force behind teaching the populace to read. Being able to read provides an individual the opportunity to learn new ideas from any source that is written.

The need to spread the word provided a need to educate and led to new ideas. Advances in science occurred in the Eight through Thirteenth century under Islamic rule. Chemistry, Mathematics, Medicine, Astronomy, and Engineering saw advancement that led to better living and understanding of the world around us.

In Islam science and philosophy were viewed holistically. During the Ninth through Thirteenth centuries, under Islamic controlled areas, there are recorded contributions to the area of automatic control systems. For example, water clocks using float valve regulators, level controls using float valves, or combination of syphon's and on-off controls. The types of mechanical controls used would not be seen in this number again until the 1800's during the industrial revolution.

The Christian church supported Astronomy as well as Mathematics and Philosophy. The findings by Copernicus, Da Vinci, and St. Augustine provided a starting point for today's Engineering, Astronomy, and Philosophy.

Copernicus discovered our place in the solar system, even if it was controversial. Da Vinci furthered healthcare by performing autopsies and carefully capturing each physical aspect through drawing and notation. St. Augustine realized that the downfall of civilizations, such as Rome, occurred when humanity looked for scapegoats and did not recognize their part in allowing corruption to occur.

Eventually the age of reason came, and the understanding that following a steady path of material and spiritual progress could exist together. Religion provided many positives we take for granted today. It was a supporting structure which brought together different cultures, and through bringing together diversity allowed cultural norms to be breached.

We can all probably agree it was not a perfect system, but religion provided relationship, kinship, education toward becoming more. What can a future in understanding look like?

Religion - Future Focus

The scientific method comes out of much of the research done during the medieval periods. Those who had to study and learn under religious piety knew discussion must occur in a non-threatening manner, or possibly face crimes of heresy. Taking a look at how we build off of this strength is probably as good as any.

Without the scientific method research would be one sided. Scientific method prescribes that we make observations, propose a hypothesis (what we think), design and perform an experiment or survey to test the null-hypothesis, analyze the data to determine whether to reject or fail to reject the null-hypothesis, and if necessary, propose and test a new hypothesis.

In research we can consider the hypothesis a trial against the null-hypothesis. The data gathered either shows the n null-hypothesis to be plausible or not plausible. If the null-hypothesis is rejected, then the hypothesis is accepted.

The main thing to remember is that we reject or fail to reject the null hypothesis. We do not prove that the null hypothesis is true and we do not accept the null hypothesis.

Religious theory at its most basic level provides ethics, morality, a sense of cohesion and tolerance. The message of religion is not the problem it is the interpretation of man that causes confusion. His Holiness the Dalai Lama provides great insight into what the future could be. With inter-religious understanding, peace between secularists and adherents, we can have a compassionate and happier humanity. Without peaceful coexistence humankind will eventually consume itself through destructive means.

Religions have played their part as a source of conflict, suffering, and human division. This does not need to be the role of religion going forward. Religion has, and can teach individuals how to live ethically, provide deeper meaning of self, and continue to provide comfort and peace in times of great tragedy.

Where are we?

Let's look at the premise we started with. Problems are past, future is where possibilities lie, build on present strengths to build a positive future. Let's review ethics and values in a business frame before moving on.

Rationalism drives truth as it exists within our minds, the value of truth is not based on experience. Rational thought is based on the complexity of the concept and will affect the value of the truth. An innate concept is not necessarily truth; it is only perception as we understand from cultural social backgrounds.

Values are clear statements of what is critically important from a cultural view point. Ethics become the vehicle for converting values into action, or doing the right thing. The virtue of ethics focuses on integrity and a belief that if the person in question has good moral character, and genuine motivation and intentions, they are behaving ethically.

Idealism is the theory that the nature of reality is based on the mind or ideas. The external world is said to exist prior to, and independent of, knowledge and consciousness. Within idealism the approach is to find the highest principles of rational understanding, and provide principles which add to ethics and aesthetics of all domains of human culture.

The theory of focusing on the rights of individuals, deontology, is about finding the highest principles in ourselves. According to deontological theory, the individual must examine their duties when making a decision. The deontological approach is based on universal principles such as honesty, fairness, justice, and respect for persons and property. Rights, such as the rights to privacy and safety, are also important.

The belief of an individual, utilitarian or deontologist, will drive their actions and moral intensity. Utilitarianism believes that as long as no one is hurt the decision is ethical. A deontologist believes strongly in fairness and respect for others. A utilitarian would be more likely to agree that assisted death of a terminally ill person is ethical while the deontologist would most likely believe this not to be fair and is disrespectful of the rights of the person. The meaning of value is different for each ethical principle, utilitarians believe euthanasia is beneficial while deontologist believe it is harmful. In this case the value of our ethics causes action or inaction.

Let us briefly examine drug companies' business practice of providing consulting fees and special incentives to doctors. On the surface it seems business as usual. Although, when the company begins requesting the doctor use their product is the doctor inclined to use the product in order to not lose the fees and other kickbacks?

It is common for doctors to receive very lucrative consulting fees from drug companies. The problem is a doctor who receives enormous consulting fees or other financial considerations may lose his or her objectivity in choosing the best treatment for their patients. It is difficult to determine whether doing harm is the intent, although how could a doctor be fair and level in dealing with patients when the doctor is 'in debt' to pharmaceutical companies.

It may not be a spoken or written contracted debt, although future consulting fees may drive the doctor to treat a patient with a drug when the drug is not actually needed. Within the context of do no harm and fairness this seems to fall into an ethical dilemma where both sides would agree this to be potentially unethical.

A Gallup poll showed that 30% of employees in America feel engaged at work. That means for every person who does feel engaged, two do not.

In review, understanding how our perception shapes reality is important to how we interface with our world. When viewing others and situations take a moment to look outside our perceptions and appreciate the strength in differences. We tend to dwell in our preconceived notions, let's work on leaving those behind.

Quotes that Matter ~ Thinking Moments

"You never know the truth. You know 'A' truth." ~ Unknown

Truth is based in our perception of the culture around us. Perceptions are driven by peer groups, parents, clubs, cities, and localities we belong to. If influences in our life taught us the only way to eat grits is with butter, salt, and pepper, we tend to believe that is the only way grits should be eaten. If we learned that sugar should go on grits then that is our reality.

Let us presume the previous is true for us, we believe grits should come with butter, salt, and pepper. Imagine traveling outside the area of our normal culture and we order grits at a restaurant. The server asks, do we want sugar with our grits.

We may think the server has made an error, maybe they misunderstood our order. The waitress confirms that in that area grits are usually eaten with sugar. We learn that grits can be eaten either way, and maybe even plain. Our truth changes, and our mindset grows, it does not mean we agree.

"If an egg is broken by an outside force, life ends. If broken by an inside force, life begins. Great things always begin from the inside." ~ Jim Kwik

The simple truth is the strongest motivation is based on our belief in our ability to achieve a task. If we believe we are good at a task and feel pride or joy in performing the task, then we are more likely to carry out the effort to achieve the objective of the task. If we believe we are not capable of achieving a task, then we are less likely to take the time to put forth any effort. There are two types of motivations at work, intrinsic and extrinsic.

Intrinsic motivation is an internal drive to accomplish a task because we either enjoy or have a strong belief in the task that needs to be performed. It is true that some tasks are difficult but once we begin a task we believe in we tend to work at it until it is completed, we may even find it fun. At times even a task we enjoy may require influence to begin.

Extrinsic motivation is an external force which encourages us to perform a task. Usually a task that we would rather not due, for example many individuals go to work because they need to, not because they want to. Encouragement can come in the form of positive or negative methods. If we go to work we earn a paycheck, if we do not go to work eventually we will get fired.

The higher the intrinsic motivation the more likely we are to perform, the focus of extrinsic motivation is to build up the intrinsic motivation and higher performance (At least it should be). The method used to motivate will have an effect on the outcome.

"I've learned that people will forget what you said, people will forget what you did, but people will never forget how you made them feel." ~ Maya Angelou

This is about relationship, perception, and also has an effect on motivation. If we decided that it would be a good thing to exercise we might go to a gym to get assistance. We go to a local Gym where we have decided to spend a few hours a week in an effort to improve ourselves. We go out, buy a new pair of shoes and outfit and are inspired by others who have shown great results. We know that exercise will help us feel better and we are ready to tackle the gym.

Upon arriving we are pointed to the equipment, we begin and realize this is work. This is the point of opportunity, either a leader steps up points us in the right direction or we just wasted a lot of time and money.

A good trainer will build up your confidence and remind you of the goal. When you falter they will tell you how well you are doing and that you can reach the goal. Through positive reinforcement your intrinsic motivation builds and you can achieve. A poor trainer will tell you how pathetic you are and destroy any motivation you had and your chance of returning is slim.

The next time we thought about exercising the negative emotion from that moment would become a barrier to starting again. Again the greatest things begin within us and through intrinsic motivation we can achieve great things.

"We judge ourselves by our intentions. And others by their actions." ~ Stephen Covey Remember that you may not be seeing the full picture before you judge others. Their intentions may not match their actions.

The indication here is that what we think may not be correct. For example, our initial thought may be that the actions of an individual is due to internal behavior and that the individual is responsible or in control of the outcome. This action is known as attribution theory which suggests that when we observe behavior, we attempt to determine if it is internally or externally caused.

What is our reaction if someone drops our cellular phone? We might ask why you did that, and assume the person did it on purpose. Another common accident seems to be the cellular phone going swimming.

In one case I recall one of my children at the beach carrying another child's cell phone. The owner of the cellular phone decided to go swimming and left it with his sibling. When I arrived upon the scene the child with the phone decided to go play Frisbee with his brother. Unfortunately, he forgot the phone was in his pocket and wound up falling into the water.

The reaction of the child who owned the phone was not one of care when he found out the phone got soaked. He did not believe it was an accident. The child who owned the phone attributed the phones destruction to an internal cause, in this case we would probably agree it may have been, although we can be relatively certain it was an accident. The sibling who owned the phone swore the other child did it on purpose. At this point the behavior and result were not attributable to the intent.

The destroyer of the phone did not intend on getting in the water, he just wanted to play on the beach with everyone else. He still had the phone in his pocket because his brother asked him to keep it with him. The playing on the beach and throwing the Frisbee attributed to him getting into the water.

Three factors assist in determining internally and externally caused behaviors. The determination depends on distinctiveness of the action, consensus of the action, consistency of the action.

Distinctiveness depends on whether an individual displays different behavior in different situations. If the difference is high in different situations, then external can be attributed. If a different behavior is low in different situations, then internal can be attributed.

Consensus depends on whether everyone in a similar situation responds relatively in the same way or not. If the response has a high outcome of occurrence opportunity, then it is externally attributable. If the response has a low outcome of occurrence opportunity, then it is internally attributable.

Consistency depends on how a person responds over time. If my child made a habit of destroying his brother's phone, then it would be considered internally attributable. If the destruction of the phone was an isolated case, then it was externally attributable.

In reflection my child does not wantonly destroy phones in many different situations. It is likely that playing Frisbee near the water can result in getting wet and my son does not go around destroying his brother's phone on a regular basis. In this case the end result is it was an externally attributable, unfortunate, accident. No malice was intended, I think.

The Appreciative Environment

Business Application

Now that we have begun to understand that focus of a situation is based on our perceptions let's take a look at how that works in business. Why should I care about an appreciative environment in business you might ask? It is commonly known that we attract like-minded individuals. Those similarities cause groupthink and interfere with creativity and innovation. To overcome this barrier to diversity and encourage better brainstorming and ideas we need to learn to appreciate differences.

Recently I read a similar idea that stated successful individuals think different. The key to their success is not complaining, they look for opportunities. Complaining fosters, a focus on what is wrong with our lives, doing so continues the cycle and others who also are focused on complaining will congregate and continue the focus. Appreciative environments build on strengths and focusing on positives and allows us to focus on what is right in our lives.

In 1919 Henry Gantt explained that the Handicraft Era of industrial progress was characterized by high manual skills. The tradesmen or craftsmen were told what was wanted, and at this point their ingenuity and skill were coupled to produce the required item. This handicraft era can also be earmarked by the lack of standardization of process, product and price. In this era the basic variables of how to produce, and what to produce were left to the individual producer and thus it was impossible to provide standards of performance and quality.

As time passed, the industrial situation evolved that was characterized by large groups of congregated labor working for wages in cottages or factories. "Cottage Production" of the time should not be confused with present day manufacturing methods, since history depicts this situation as a grouping of tradesmen or handi-crafters each producing a finished product, rather than the subdivision of tasks to a-highly repetitive chore, aided and abetted by machinery and controlled methods.

The distinguishing features of this cottage production were congregated labor and product specifications existed, but without detailed instructions in method or standardized conditions.

In the 18th century the Industrial Revolution occurred changing the interface between producer and consumer. The producer was now distant from the consumer. At the same time the task of the individual was reduced from completing a product to that of producing a component, or in many instances to a single operation on a component. This created the simultaneous need for both the designer of a product from an overall standpoint, as well as that of a coordinator of manufacturing.

Inherent in this evolution of industrial progress was the specialization of skills. The first-line foreman was chosen for his position on the basis of his wide experience and skill in producing, while at the same time the product designer progressed through drafting and detailing work.

This quite naturally left a void in the organization for those who might appreciate equally the problems of both design and production. Why should we care? Because, understanding the evolution of industry helps us to see difficulties in change and the reason for change.

Frederick Winslow Taylor

Taylor the Tyrant -Past Focus

In 1873 Europe & North America was in an economic financial crisis. The financial crisis ran into 1879 although the after effect on the U.S. during the age of industrialization caused the workforce to be wary of management.

The Workers written by Walter A. Wyckoff in 1898 provides insight into the philosophy of the time. The workers of that time had an unspoken agreement of what constituted a day's labor. A man could fall below the quota although it was taboo to go above the quota. The fear was that by going above a certain amount of labor would provide management an opportunity to require more work for less pay. Another effect of going above quota was the fear of losing jobs.

Taylor called the work method followed natural and systemic soldering. Natural soldering was based on the natural laziness of the laborer and systemic was the thoughtfulness of the laborers toward each other.

Systemic soldering kept each man from working more than the perceived norm. Change was not welcome especially if it was focused in any direction toward increasing effort and reducing pay.

The perception of the laborer is important to understand before we discuss Frederick Taylor. Frederick Taylor worked as a gang boss (Foreman) in the Midvale Steel factory during the late 1800's. He felt the workers' method of soldering was wrong and that it needed to change. While in charge of the machinist he told them he knew they could perform at a higher output level and that he was going to make sure they did.

Taylor believed that the soldering of the machinist was a $1/3^{rd}$ of the actual ability they should be able to accomplish. He went about the task of training the machinist and expecting them to provide higher outputs. He offered up piece rate incentives to encourage the higher output. Taylor decreased the pay per piece in an attempt to coerce the workforce into having to perform at the higher output to earn their standard pay.

Taylor was thought of as an angry, bullheaded combative individual. The labor force went as far as breaking machines in retaliation to Taylor's quota expectations. Taylor instituted a fine system for broken machines. His approach to working with others caused many to see him as tactless and pugnacious, including those who called him friend. No wonder the workforce was resistant to follow or trust Taylor's motives.

Taylor the Thoughtful - Present Focus

It is easy to look at Frederick Taylor and the Midvale machinist episode as a confrontation of management against worker. In order to understand it is important to know more about Taylor. In 1874, when the financial crisis was hitting the labor force hard, Taylor went into a patternmaker apprenticeship with Enterprise Hydraulic Works of Philadelphia. He started out without any wages and after four years, in 1878, he was earning $3 per week.

In 1878 he was able to find work at Midvale Steel as a common laborer. He worked his way from laborer up to chief engineer while at Midvale Steel. During this time, he saw the poor relationship between management and laborer. He understood that the laborer was not valued and management had created an ineffective piece work incentive system. Midvale believed the workers could control their own behavior and be self-motivated to produce at higher rates of output.

Taylor attempted to alter the perception of the workforce. He worked to show that the rate of output could be increased through standardization of the method. Taylor also believed that by producing at a higher rate the workforce could earn more pay. As output increased the factory would earn more and thus the laborer would share in the profit. Taylor's motivation was not in increasing the output for the sake of the company alone but for the workforce as well.

The traditional method of incremental piece rate pay paid workers a standard wage. The standard paid the same for work up to the quota of standard output. Taylor's differential piece rate system set a standard that must be met to be paid a full wage. On the surface this looks as negative because less efficient workers are paid less for not meeting standard while those who meet standard are paid a full wage. Although, those who perform at a higher output could earn a higher wage by exceeding the standard.

Taylor learned from his experience with the machinist that he could not coerce the workforce into higher output. Cutting pay per piece and fines were received poorly and created further strife between management and laborer. Taylor eventually won over the machinist through the differential piece rate system, training, and standardized tasks. Never again would he utilize fines and rate cuts, or punishment, to accomplish gains.

Taylor further learned from this experience that to overcome soldering he needed to come up with standards through scientific studies. Taylor set out after this experience to monitor how work was performed, how long a task should take, and how many steps made up a job.

His methods helped to put in place operations standards that provided clear guidelines of what it took to perform a given task. His contributions helped to improve the rate at which labor accomplished work by decreasing unnecessary steps, developing new tools, proper training of the labor force, an almost equal division of the work responsibility between the laborer and management.

In the past management placed all the burden of how to accomplish the task on the laborer, now management focuses more on providing encouragement and removing barriers to accomplishing the job.

The method, scientific management, drove two ideas through the planning and operation functions to increase efficiency and the effectiveness of workers, which would provide an increase to profits. The two ideas were to increase efficiency through process methods and provide a better sharing of profit (rewards) with the workforce. The focus was mainly on task completion and how to increase completion of tasks consistently, on time, to a standardized process.

Behavioral studies indicate that understanding what is expected of us, being properly trained, and rewarded in line with what we value contributes to job satisfaction. Job Satisfaction is one of the criteria which contributes to higher performance in the work place.

Taylor set the scene for developments in many business functions and disciplines including: accounting cost control, compensation management, human resources management, organized labor relations, operations process control management, operations service sector management, quality management, and technology management.

Peter Drucker pointed out that under Taylor's methods production increased "fifty-fold". The introduction of scientific management set in place what an expected work day should look like. During this period of time productivity methods improved and quality output of production increased. These management methods were devised to help management improve the efficiency and measure output of the worker. During the 1900's this was the intellectual property which management had at their disposal to improve production and service.

Taylor introduced three questions. Was there one best way of doing things? Could some elements of work be eliminated or parts of the operation combined? Could the sequences of the processes be improved? By answering these questions management could plan how to best utilize labor.

Taylor & Scientific Management – Future Focus

Taylor's methods provide us with a few lessons. Management must manage the work and set out the tasks to be performed. The workforce needs to have a clear understanding of the process and their standard requirement to perform. The workforce needs to believe they can perform, and if necessary be trained to perform. Management needs to provide clear feedback on how the individual is performing and determine if further training is required. The reward needs to be in line with what the worker perceives to be of value for the work performed.

The standard put in place for each task was toward a rate that an individual suited fort eh position could perform and thrive. The focus was on long term wellbeing of the laborer and their ability to have a long prosperous work career instead of being overworked and wore out in a short period of time.

These methods standards Taylor focused on persist within job design. Set tasks to a level that an average person can attain the expectations. Overworking the individual physically or mentally will cause cognitive withdrawal and lead to poor job satisfaction.

Critics look may look at Taylor's methods as being biased toward management, but the standardization provide a clear level of expectations for the individual employee. His methods provide management & leadership the ability to set clear procedural expectations and assist new and current employees stay up to date with job requirements. An individual has the right to know what is expected and how to perform to meet the standard.

Whereas originally Scientific Management took empowerment away going forward it has provided a clear path to empowerment. Today the workforce is better educated and can follow standards provided.

Employees can point to the standard and notice readily when task is adjusted from the norm. Parameters can be set which help employees adjust their methods to meet customers' needs internally and externally.

Out of Taylor's change to production through scientific management we have several important concepts. As we focus on the opportunities provided we have better definition and allocation of tasks to be performed under standard conditions. Process analysis of functional work to be performed leading to clear procedures. Management has direction in the form of planning, cost control, compensation for standard output, training of new employees, and labor relations importance.

It seems to me that Taylor put in place the opportunity to make management practices more scientific, and to make them more humane. In the end Taylor's real focus was on the individual and improving their position.

George Elton Mayo

Mayo in the Dark – Past Focus

In 1924 Elton Mayo was hired by Westinghouse to study work conditions in their Hawthorne plant. Engineers felt the illumination of the work area may have an effect of performance. Mayo manipulated work conditions of two groups of workers in an effort to explore conditions of groups in the workplace due to illumination in the factory.

Critics point to the research as flawed due to flexible variables and conditions presented during the study. During the study those who participated were paid higher wages; received rest periods that workers did not normally receive; and the duration of work was shortened. Workers in the study were allowed to leave their work station without obtaining permission.

Illumination levels would be set high then gradually decrease until the study group could barely see. The preferred treatment of the workers continued causing others in the plant to reject those workers socially. Critics also point to the manipulation of the variables when discussing the worker output.

The group increased output during the time in the study. Mayo's Human Relations Theory stated that each individual is unique and their behavior determines the way he or she works. Mayo postulated that the relations were more important the pay to improve worker output. Although one of the main variables adjusted for the test group was higher pay.

Here we see a manipulation of research methods and changing variables that are not part of the study. Critics point to those variable as the reason the output increased. Research is about discovery of the environment in its natural state. If the variable are manipulated which effect the environment then it is not possible to examine the natural environment.

If we are to believe the critics, Mayo manipulated a study away from its intent in order to prove his own preconceived notions of Human Relations Theory.

Elton Mayo on Target – Present Focus

As we have discussed in other examples it is easy to believe the negative. Once we are on the negative train of thought we can jump to conclusions and our perceptions build barriers to the truth.

Elton Mayo and his team realized that production increased no matter how they manipulated the variables. The lighting, except total darkness, had no effect on output. Questions were raised by Mayo and his team as to why this occurred. Between 1928 and 1930 approximately 21,000 people were interviewed to explore human behavior at work. The outcome of the questioning led to another round of experimentation called the Bank wiring observation room experiments, and ran from 1931 to 1932.

During this study pay was based on the incentive pay plan, pay increased as output increased. Researchers observed output stayed fairly constant.

The end result of the Hawthorne studies indicated that workers were reacting to and performing at a high rate due to being observed. The workers were reacting to the increased attention they were receiving, and their performance expectations and norms increased. The significance of the Hawthorne Studies showed that observation and taking an interest in the employee had a stronger impact on output.

This was a significant shift in theory. Human Relations Approach took us from forcing an individual to perform through coercion, to focusing on the well-being of an employee may provide increased output to accomplish tasks.

Elton Mayo the Light – Future Focus

Before the Hawthorne Studies, based on Frederick Taylor's Scientific Management, it was believed that individual human behavior could be corrected and controlled. The only way to increase production and increase output before the Hawthorne studies was to perfect the methods performed to increase production.

The studies showed that social complexities affected organizational life. The studies showed leaders can negatively affect followers' motivation due to poor relationship building abilities. Ineffective leaders fail to instill creativity, socialization, and rationalization in decision making.

When leaders focus on why processes are not working they create barriers. These barriers affect performance, team building, culture, and change efforts. When leaders focus on what is working and communicate a forward positive future, barriers can decrease and provide opportunities for higher performance, team functionality, strong cultures, and improved change efforts.

Leaders, based on ability to perform, communicate, and conscientiousness, have an effect on an employee's job satisfaction which impacts motivation, production, and ultimately success of the individual and the organization.

Leaders require social intelligence to create a culture within the organization for the acquisition of knowledge sharing. Acquisition begins with the assumption that social behavior is intelligent and is mediated by perception, memory, reasoning, and problem solving. Social intelligence encompasses problem solving (emotional intelligence) and problem solving evaluation (appreciative intelligence).

Problem solving requires rationalization, critical thinking, and the ability to evaluate the problem through the gathering of information in a forward thinking manner, although subjective social intelligence seems affect the cognitive process and determine how features of a situation will be perceived and interpreted.

Research indicates appreciative environments created through leaderships understanding of positive elements to create a better future may provide better outcomes and increased job satisfaction. Leaders have an effect on follower's job satisfaction. Leader's effect how task and relationship is balanced and the effect on follower's job satisfaction that can lead to high performing individuals and teams.

Management Theory continued

This process would not be complete if we didn't spend time trying to tie these concepts together and how they affect business. The following discussing is a little history, a little present, restates some of the previous material, although the end result this author wishes to provide is future opportunities.

In 1945 the Ohio State Studies brought together Scientific Management and the Human relations movement by exploring two-factor concepts of leadership behavior. The Ohio State Studies showed that those followers who were high in consideration by their leaders were more satisfied and motivated to perform and had a higher respect for the leadership.

The studies were largely ignored until 1992 when a review 160 studies showed that initiating structure and consideration were associated with effective leadership. The Ohio State Studies showed that by focusing on structure (task orientation) and People (consideration) is where management should focus. Focus on output is preferred to focus on input, especially in a diverse workforce.

Although Scientific Management is not the first theory of management it is an evolutionary step which may have provided the foundation for behavioral theory, transitional, and modern theory of management. Taylor's work provided the ground work to set methods and standardized practice in place.

Mary Parker Follett built onto Taylor's work with her research on teams. Follett's research showed that only through integrated teams, which worked toward finding a solution that was mutually agreed upon by both parties, could a successful outcome occur. This means that only through positive conflict and negotiation and arriving at resolution could teams be successful.

Follett's work opened the door for Maslow, Herzberg, and Alderfer in building models of employee needs in the workplace. The transition management era is most recognized by Peter Drucker's work on Management by Objective (MBO), which is a structured tool that sets goals for an organization.

Victor Vroom's expectancy theory utilizes goal setting theory. An employee must know how to accomplish a task. Each task (goal) is identified as a strategic or operational goal by management and employees and agreed upon. These goals are then measured and adjusted as needed to meet successful outcomes and achieve the goals. Leadership provides clear feedback on achievement and provides reward that meet the employee's expectations (reward should be something the employee values).

Sociotechnical systems are made up of four elements, innovation, communication channels, time, and the social system. Innovation is the ability to adopt an idea, practice, or project and use it in a manner not utilized before. Everett M. Rogers stated that innovation's consequences may create uncertainty and "changes that occur in an individual or a social system as a result of the adoption or rejection of an innovation".

Communication is the channels which information is transferred via individuals or organizations. Methods of communication may be oral, written, or non-verbal and are hindered by the filtering and method of transferring that communication. According to Rogers time is ignored by behavioral theory although the process of entering a market and being successful is driven by the entry to market. The innovator, early adopter, and early majority have an edge in market success and that later adopters and laggards are less aware of knowledge innovation. The social system is a set of interrelated units or cross-functional team, which work jointly to solve a problem. The nature of the social system affects individual's ability to innovate and work together to solve problems.

The sociotechnical theories of Rogers and the historical management and behavioral theories provide a good understanding of work systems situation. Sociotechnical work system is comprised of individuals interacting with a technical subsystem. The technical subsystem is the process, equipment, tools needed to perform the work. The employee subsystem is the people (or Individual) needed to perform the work. Both of the subsystems are required in order for an organization to be successful.

Research has shown that there is a relationship between an appreciative environment and an employee's job satisfaction. Leadership has as direct impact on employees' perception of the appreciative environment.

The subjects of the study represented employees in service industry, manufacturing, and retail trade within small business operations. The research showed to be pertinent to small businesses but also has an impact on how leadership in any business can build high performing teams. The results indicate that leadership and individuals have the ability to contribute to high performing teams.

Thinking Moment: *Here is a simple exercise to try. Think of a colleague, friend, or family member and write down one positive thought. Make it something that really meant something to you. The next time you have a confrontational opportunity, look at what you wrote down before having the discussion. How you proceed will be the difference between positive and negative outcomes.*

- Survey results indicate that an appreciative environment is important to followers' job satisfaction and has an impact on whether they will have a tendency toward being motivated, absentee, and accept change activities.

- Implementation of programs to increase leadership's ability to relate to followers is important to create a positive appreciative environment.

Multiple Intelligences

It is important to understand there is more than one type of intelligence. More than on intelligence type means we each have strengths in different areas and each contributes in a different manner. There are at least eight intelligences, musical-rhythmic, visual-spatial, Verbal-linguistic, logical-mathematical, bodily-kinesthetic, interpersonal, intrapersonal, and naturalistic.

Multiple intelligence also includes intelligence quotient (IQ) in logical-mathematical, appreciative intelligence within linguistics (the ability to convince others to take a course of action), social intelligence within interpersonal (the ability to perceive moods, intentions, motivations, and feelings in others), and emotional intelligence within intrapersonal (self-knowledge, ability to understand oneself).

Intelligence is the ability or cognitive sense to understand how to do something. In learning, the higher the intelligence (IQ) the faster an individual is able to reach cognition.

General mental ability (GMA) or intelligence quotient, in correlation with conscientiousness has shown to have an impact on job performance. General mental ability is important because it has an impact on the rate or openness to knowledge consumption. The ability of an individual to achieve interpersonal or intrapersonal cognition is tied to our general mental ability.

Intelligence is more than general mental ability it is the knowledge of how to drive effectiveness and efficiency in business. Intelligence quotient may provide a determinant of a person's ability to understand and learn, although if intelligence quotient alone was all that is required to succeed logic would direct that organizations need only hire the best and brightest and they will succeed.

As early as 1918 Charles Mann (A Study of Engineering Education) provided survey evidence that 85% of financial success is due to leaderships' personality, communication, negotiation, and ability to lead.

The research, performed by Carnegie Institute of Technology, showed ability was more important than intelligence quotient or general mental ability alone and that only 15% of success was due to technical ability (Mann, 1918).

During this period of time Frederick Taylor's Scientific Management placed many industrial organizations focus on task and job design. The focus on task and job design diffused the focus on relationship in America. During the early 1900's the United States was more interested in how to get more work out of an individual and how to coordinate efforts across multiple cultures. The United States predominant work force was Italians, Irish, Germans, and English speaking individuals all in the same production facilities. For the era breaking tasks to their lowest level possible helped to define effort required to accomplish objectives.

Intelligence, or general mental ability, in the form of intelligence quotient is the driving force behind innovative ideas and the ability to solve complex problems.

Intelligence quotient alone has not proven to be the catalyst to good leadership and the creation of an environment conducive to organizational commitment, motivation, and productive employees. Leaders need to be conscientious to create opportunities to motivate employees in unstructured innovative atmospheres. In a structured environment employees know the process clearly, little support is needed to help drive success. In the unstructured situation employees need leadership to create opportunities to share ideas openly and to be free from reprisal. The ability of the leader to be open minded, creates an atmosphere conducive to free exchange, and to rationally pick a direction requires multiple intelligences.

The use of multiple intelligence and adjusting conflict styles between integrating, compromising, obliging, in an effort to create a free exchange of ideas produces a direct effect on job performance.

Creative intelligence, cognition, prior knowledge, imagination, energy, and awareness are required for developing entrepreneurial opportunities. Multiple intelligence is a factor in relatedness and influence and helps to increase creativeness.

Howard Gardner (1993) questioned ability and learning as a structured cognitive development which followed a standard path. Knowledge builds at different rates depending on experience and cognitive ability. Intelligences are multivariate; Robert Sternberg (1997) discussed triarchic theory as a general theory of human intelligence. Intelligence is composed of analytical, creative, and practical abilities which are part of the framework for practical emotional and social intelligence. This triarchic theory view of intelligence breaks into three forms of intelligence which provide us a framework for interface with employees through solving problems (creative), evaluating problems (analytic), and knowledge acquisition (practical ability).

Multiple intelligence spans more than general mental ability, it is the interpersonal, intrapersonal, sense making abilities of a leader and each individual to make informative decisions which have an effect on performance. It is our ability to use those intelligences to understand the workforce, the work, and the situation to motivate followers, our peers, and team members in a direction to accomplish tasks.

Why should we care about AE?

Why should we care about creating an Appreciative Environment? As discussed our own perceptions can lead us in negative directions. Negative directions lead to poor team and work environments. Poor environments lead to low performance and barriers to creativity and innovation. To move forward it is important we understand how management and leadership is perceived. While the terms leader and manager have diversely different functional roles, for our purpose the terms are interchangeable due to the impact these roles have on the organization.

Leaders set the tone of an organization and depending on the circumstances, leaders come from anywhere. Leaders can be managers, although not all managers are leaders. Leaders are not necessarily a formal position, they come from those willing to step up and take action. While reading this remember we all can be leaders. The following is provided to guide your insight, so you can be a leader when needed.

The history of management and leadership thought has explored two main interfaces between the leader and the follower. The two elements are the task to be accomplished and the relationship between the leader and the follower. As discussed earlier, Taylor focused on the task being performed and the expectation of management on the laborer. The laborer was not provided clear direction and the task was not clearly defined. Management had no way to measure expectations and therefore the workforce set the tone through soldiering.

Research has also shown that followers perceive a positive effect on job satisfaction due to an appreciative environment created by leadership. Job satisfaction is an important concept due to its role in job design, change initiatives, leadership and employees quitting. Examination of social, emotional, and appreciative intelligence through the lenses of major researchers on these topics is focused on a relation to appreciative intelligence and job satisfaction.

Early management and industrial psychology addressed three main problems; finding the right worker for the job, matching the worker to the job based on the analysis of the job, and the retention of the worker following hiring. Current focus should be on whether the work population experiences an appreciative environment. Appreciative Environment encompasses Job satisfaction and can contribute as a predictor of intention to quit and cognitive job withdrawal.

One of the main drivers of withdrawal is change in direction, policy, and operations. The global economic environment changes quickly and companies that pay attention to the effects of change and how to reset individual's expectations positively will perform better.

Withdrawal and quitting after a change in the organization is a result of followers not being engaged in the change and refusing, either psychologically or methodically, to change.

Utilizing socialization methods which build the appreciative environment has a positive impact in creating organizational commitment. When the organization intent is not believed to be genuine then dissatisfaction and low commitment can be the outcome. An appreciative environment focuses on building on present strength to build a positive possible future and decreasing the barriers to change.

Thinking Moment: *Why we should care about retention, culture, and change buy-in within the organization. The knowledge that our employees hold is an asset in the form of human capital. There is an expense to the organization in retraining when we lose human capital. Employees who stay on the job but withdraw and perform at lower levels can also be a drain on resources. Socialization has shown to have a positive affect when the process is applied properly. Successful change efforts include stake holders and create an atmosphere of inclusion through open exchange of information. Part of the process requires early notification of the reason and need for change and how it affects the stakeholders.*

In addition to job satisfaction the Appreciative Environment concept is tied to three types of intelligence philosophies, appreciative intelligence (AI), emotional intelligence (EI), and social intelligence (SI). Culture is driven through socialization although should not require the loss of individuality. Every organization has a unique culture. Some choose to ignore it, others try to defy it, and wise leaders will attempt to understand it. Why? Because organizational culture can have an impact on the organization's ability to implement a strategy, introduce new technology, or increase productivity.

By paying attention, active listening, leadership and team members can get more positive results and interaction. Appreciative Environment is the ability to reframe, appreciate the positive, and reframe thinking toward the future.

Appreciative Environment focuses on the positive stories during the discovery phase to decrease the resistance to change and diminish barriers created through defense of prior activities.

Social intelligence is part of building the social relationship which is an important concept which allows discussion of the future without bringing up the past. Leaders are responsible to create an atmosphere of belonging through social interaction which increases the ability of the employee to engage and adapt. An important part of this engagement should be reinforcing that mistakes happen and punitive actions are not a result.

Emotional intelligence is part of rational ability to decide which knowledge approach may be the best direction based on the circumstances. An ability to interact with a diverse employee population, a complex environment, and multifaceted decisions require leaders and followers to have a fully developed emotional presence. Emotional intelligence has a significant effect on leader-member exchange and increased relationship between leadership and followers in a positive manner.

In the field of intelligences there has not traditionally been a connection among the related constructs. The Appreciative Environment model, we will discuss later, is an attempt to show how to integrate social intelligence (SI), emotional intelligence (EI), and cultural intelligence (CQ) in a manner that they work together to create an appreciative environment (AE). Researchers have acknowledged and agree that it is important to understand intelligence concepts in a new light. Appreciative Environment is that new light.

EI and SI have shown in research cases to have a positive effect on the work environment and job satisfaction. AI studies have shown to have a strong correlation to creating positive job satisfaction. This relationship helps us better understand how each construct may be related to important organizational outcomes, such as barriers to change, and cognitive withdrawal of employees (followers).

During the first half of the 1900's, Edward Thorndike measured the mental capacity toward social constructs.

Social Intelligence was considered a single concept until neuroscientist helped to define social intelligence as two personal intelligences, interpersonal (Social) and intrapersonal (Self) intelligences.

Interpersonal intelligence is the ability to read others, and that intrapersonal is the ability to access one's own feelings. Having the ability to read others is social intelligence, the ability to understand our own feelings is emotional intelligence. Studies have shown that a person does not have to be able to read others in order to be in tune with their own feelings. Although in order to read others an individual must also be in tune with their own feelings. This reinforces the concept that if we do not understand who we are we cannot know our place in society, teams, or organizations.

The construct of appreciative intelligence is the ability to reframe our assessment of situations, taking into consideration positive aspects, and see a path to the future. Appreciative intelligence requires an understanding of the current situation through open minded inquiry.

The process is about seeing the reality of everyday events, and consciously or unconsciously redefining the problems facing the organization, focusing forward to a new future and a desired goal, and seeing ways to present possibilities that could be used. Appreciative Intelligence practices are designed according to one general accepted procedure, namely implementing the 4-D Cycle: Discovery, Dream, Design, and Delivery/Destiny.

Job satisfaction is the measure of how much a person enjoys or identifies with their job. This is expressed through the antecedents of job satisfaction. The overall job is evaluated based on work attributes such as the work being meaningful, creative, satisfying, interesting, and challenging. Learning organizations can enhance job satisfaction of employees through building a shared vision, personal mastery, and systematic cooperation, external and internal satisfaction.

Social intelligence is the ability to sense others and create an atmosphere of trust and belonging. Emotional intelligence is the ability to think rationally, be self-aware, and be creative. Appreciative intelligence is the analytical ability to be open to creative thinking, innovative ideas, and forward thinking. Appreciative environment is created by reframing how we view ourselves, others, and situations.

Job satisfaction has an effect on an organizations' operational focus and performance, an appreciative environment has shown a positive impact on job satisfaction and can lead to high performing organizations.

Leadership

As a leader, whether formal or informal, it is important we have a cognizant understanding of our effect on individual's abilities to perform.

Leaders require social intelligence to create a culture within the organization for the acquisition of knowledge sharing. Acquisition begins with the assumption that social behavior is intelligent and is mediated by perception, memory, reasoning, and problem solving. Social intelligence encompasses problem solving (emotional intelligence) and problem solving evaluation (appreciative intelligence) and should be sensitive to the situation.

Problem solving requires rationalization, critical thinking, and the ability to evaluate the problem through the gathering of information in a forward thinking manner, although subjective social intelligence may affect the cognitive process and determine how features of a situation will be perceived and interpreted. Being in tune and thoughtful of our actions has an effect on others.

Leadership establishes a culture, culture is the shared values, beliefs, and perceptions held by followers in an organization. Leaderships approach and management of followers occurs by focusing on either task or relationship. Task oriented focus evolves in a predominantly hierarchy type organization, relationship oriented focus evolves from a predominantly clan type organization. In 2003 Daulatram Lund surveyed organizational types to determine the effect the type of organization may have on job satisfaction. In 2011 Yuan Tsai followed up and researched the relationship between organizational culture, leadership behavior, and job satisfaction. The studies showed leadership behavior has a direct effect on employee job satisfaction.

Studies also showed a positive correlation between organization type and job satisfaction. Comparisons of types showed that Clan type organizations had the highest job satisfaction, hierarchy type organizations had the lowest job satisfaction.

Although the research also showed that cultures which align with followers belief in the culture, perform better and exhibit good job satisfaction. The finding was consistent across all organization types Clan, Adhocracy, Hierarchy, and Market.

Why is that important? Because this means that in any culture the main driver is the ability of leadership has a direct effect on individual behaviors. Job Satisfaction was positively affected by leadership's open communication, better coordination of process, and avoiding negative conflict situations. How we handle conflict is important, conflict is not bad but negative conflict is always destructive to the individual and the team.

Thinking Moment: Think of a situation where a team member states an off the cuff thought believing they are funny. Others in the team may blow it off although some may not see the humor. Due to our backgrounds, culturally and other, these our opportunities for teams to fall apart. Leadership needs to create an atmosphere that allows team members the ability to say openly how they feel about such situations. A positive conversation and learning opportunity should occur to assist others in recognizing how we all may make others feel. This is the beginning of our reframing and helping others reframe to create an appreciative environment. We will discuss more about reframing in the model.

Leadership is concerned with sustained industry and defining the industry focus to allow a sharing of the profit pool, internally and externally, and creates an integrative focus. Business competition should be rigorous but not ruinous allowing companies to compete for market share in the same general market, although not attempt to dominate the market. Companies may fair better by competing for a specific niche, and not compete on dominance across markets or price.

Similar to German management which focuses on a similar method called Leistungswettbewerb, competition based on the basis of excellence in their product and services. Quality will begin to suffer if companies compete on price alone, eventually leading to a collapse. Employee job satisfaction and increased performance can help reduce costs and increase profits without effecting the overall market share.

Focusing on strategy and how to be effective and not ruinous is a good start although once strategy is in place it is important to understand strategy is not stagnant and should be a fluid process. Strategy has emerged over the last century to provide formal systems and standards for strategic analysis. In the process of building the depth of the strategic model breadth has been lost. Focus should be on strategy at the beginning, setting the tone for the vision and mission of the organization. As competition and market forces change adaptation in the organization is required due to constant shifts in the environment.

Leadership effects the organization through job design, motivation, and creating positive or negative atmosphere that causes followers to hold high or low organizational commitment. All organizations should embrace social teaming and relationship building to combat current and future shifts in industry. Leaders need to be able to create and maintain employee commitment and flexibility toward good relations with key stakeholders, and focus on the future.

Separation of strategic direction and operations is important. The Chief Executive Officer (CEO) is the one who sets a company's identity and is responsible for delegating certain responsibilities while retaining responsibility for industry competitiveness. If the CEO is to continue strategy, then the communication with leadership must be fluid. Strategy with leadership must be adaptive and allow the organization to adjust, at the same time the CEO must be aware of the industry and drive policies which support this new direction. If the CEO is busy trying to run operations, then important strategic decisions at an industry level may be overlooked.

The CEO should perform as the guardian of the organizational purpose; watching, guiding, and bringing it back to its center, even as the center evolves. The job of the strategist cannot be outsourced because the work is never done and why the CEO must perform the function continuously.

Leaders are not always in formal positions and come from non-traditional sources. Organizations may not recognize the leaders they need because they may come from employees not in traditional formal leadership roles. Change occurs so rapidly that one leader cannot hope to keep abreast of all the changes. This seems a logical thought and observation especially when we review the structure of large organizations where the CEO and top level management are separated from the day to day activities of the operations.

The CEO is responsible for the strategy, although the leadership is responsible for the ongoing operations of the organization. It is impossible for traditional leadership to be everywhere which means that leadership must be developed formally and informally which is capable of driving the organization to the strategy and recognize when new directions require executive level management to provide new strategic focus. These opportunities come through self-managed teams, specialist roles, and one off projects where an individual's expertise makes them an added value to leading.

Sun Tzu, a Chinese general from around 400 B.C. implemented strategies which included understanding your enemy, exploiting weaknesses and strengths, offensive strategy, maneuverability, and other strategies which helped the General gain many victories and become a great warlord. Sun Tzu's tactics are still used in military strategy today, and out of those strategies business concepts of strategy have evolved. Just as in war and battles there is competition to overcome, the same holds true in business.

In relation to Sun Tzu's methodologies we are provided a plan of taking advantage of weaknesses, flanking the competitor, and using strengths of an organization to succeed. Top level management should continue to adapt strategy which is flexible. Strategy should provide leadership direction that comes from various sources within the organization, which provides for flexibility and strength by taking advantage of the right person's skills at the right time.

The Appreciative Environment approach creates an inclusive socialized approach, and helps increase organizations learning and understanding of individuals within the organization.

The organization may find issues evolve differently, although members have insight, through preparation and practice of possible scenarios. This creates a higher level of social intelligence which helps the organization and leadership know how employees will respond. Without preparation for alternative futures, organizations may not be prepared to capitalize on opportunities or respond to threats from the external environment. Rational and creative thought provides opportunities to thoughtfully frame the alternatives to select the best course of action.

Studies show that communication and promoting the organizational vision have an influence on followers work behavior and attitudes. When management interacts with followers, creates clear mission statements and objectives, job satisfaction increases.

Knowledge

Intellectual property of an organization is in the form of human capital and is a resource to an organization. Human capital contributes to the company's intellectual property through the knowledge employees possess. The human elements of companies have gone through a change in the 20th century from laborer to knowledge worker. In the late 1800's and early 1900's the shift from agriculture to industrialized nation created a need for a management structure that could transition the masses into industrial workers. This brought about a new breed of scientific thinkers such as Fredrick Taylor, Max Weber, and Henri Fayol. The new method of scientific management was needed to increase productivity and create effective methods to manage work and workers.

Intellectual property is no longer contained solely within management. Employees are an intellectual asset.

Intellectual property is composed of human capital; human capital is the knowledge an individual holds which a company may profit from when utilized. Drucker (1999) introduced the concept that the knowledge worker should have the autonomy and responsibility for their own production. This production may be the output of material in a production or service oriented capacity. This implies that the knowledge worker has information which is needed by the company, and if allowed to use the knowledge the company will benefit.

Thinking Moment: We put a team together, brainstorm ideas, develop an action plan and our project woefully fails. What could have gone wrong? We have the team, we developed an approach, and we put a plan in place that addressed the "problem" that needed addressed. The underlying issue is commonly poor execution. When executing a plan, it is important to remember Drucker's message. In today's culture of business our employees are diverse, knowledgeable, and each has a need to feel they matter. Kurt Lewin, John Kotter, and a number of organizational change coaches have shown it is important to get buy in. Buy in does not mean approval it means working with stakeholders to understand the real problem. Management knows something is broken but they don't know why. The stakeholders are the knowledge source of how the work is done now, why it is done that way, and in many cases have ideas on what could work better. Including the stakeholders and involving them in the process builds buy in and will help champion the change.

Leaders Affect on Followers Job Satisfaction

Organizational Behavior concepts of task and relationship focus on the interface between leadership and followers. Task orientation is primarily focusing on the task to be performed and delineating the roles and specific tasks to each employee.

The task-oriented leader creates policies and procedures, informs subordinates of these procedures and develops criteria for evaluating successful employee performance. Task-oriented leaders may organize their time around a schedule of events that must be completed for each day.

Relationship-oriented leaders often act as mentors to their subordinates. They schedule time to talk with employees and incorporate their feedback into decisions. They also often try to make the work experience enjoyable and attempt to foster a positive work environment or group dynamic.

The Hawthorne Studies conducted at Westinghouse Hawthorne plant in Chicago from 1924 to 1933 helped to bring to light how relationships may have an effect on employees' Performance.

The Model

Back to my earlier comment "the ability of an individual to achieve interpersonal or intrapersonal cognition is tied to our general mental ability." This is an important item, because it tells us that each of us take a different amount of time to learn but it does not mean we cannot learn.

Practice and cognitive focus on wanting to be better at building teams and then helping others learn begins with a mentor or coach who can teach the method. Let's begin the process by examining what we have read, and focus on the next steps that follow. Some of the material is a summary of the previous sections to help keep that focus.

The figure included here is to assist in visualizing the concept presented on past, present, and future focus. Appreciative Environment is a concept built on the philosophy of finding strengths of the present to build toward future positive opportunities.

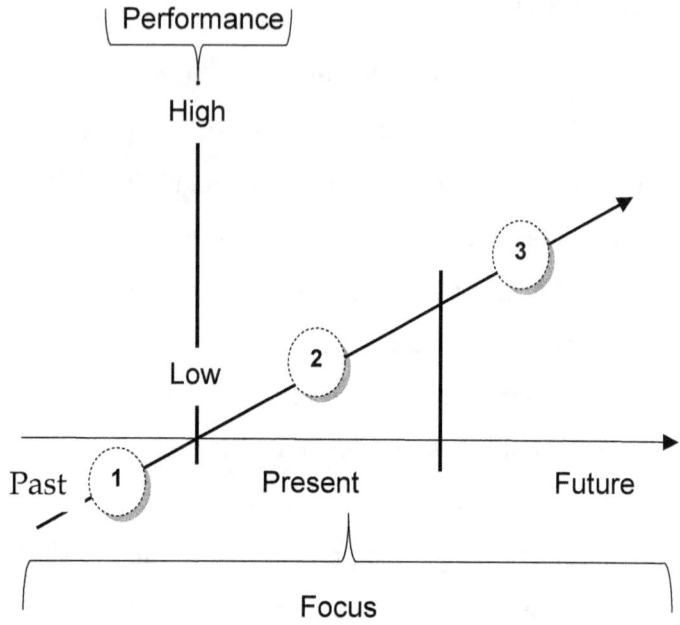

Figure 1

Legend

1. **Problems are Past**
2. **Future is Possibilities**
3. **Built on Present Strengths**

Dwelling on the past places barriers to building on present strengths and building toward possible positive futures. Organizations which create a positive focus and create intrinsic motivation build higher participation and organizational commitment.

Building the Appreciative Environment encompasses multiple intelligences. Research has shown that Social Intelligence, Emotional Intelligence, and Cultural Intelligence are interrelated concepts. Social intelligence is an overarching theory which encompasses Emotional Intelligence and Cultural Intelligence. Without cultural alignment, and interpersonal knowledge, one cannot be in tune with others feelings.

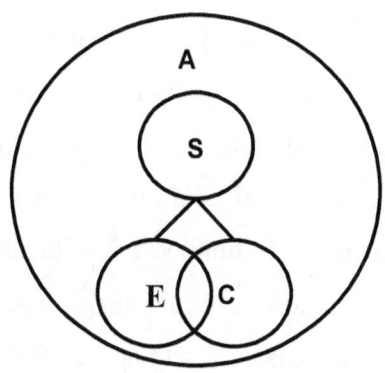

Figure 2

Legend

AE: Appreciative Environment
SI: Social Intelligence
EI: Emotional Intelligence
CQ: Cultural Intelligence

Emotional intelligence affects employees view toward a pleasant work environment, effective management, and organizational improvement. Prior research has shown that leaderships EI & SI can have a positive effect on the work environment and job satisfaction. EI & SI focus on the intrapersonal and interpersonal focus of individuals and has an effect on groups and teams' abilities to perform. The main focus of SI is the interrelation of teams and how they get along. In order to embrace SI a person must first have locus of control. The problem with social intelligence alone is its singular focus allows the individual to take on the aspects of the group and, in doing so, give up their identity.

The better in tune we are with each other, situations, and how cultural background drives our perceptions the easier it is to appreciate each individual for the strengths they bring to the organization. Each individual within an organization has the ability to positively or negatively affect performance of those they lead, follow, and/or work with. Human nature causes us to look for like individuals and overlook those who are different.

Finding the strength of even the annoying coworker, the arrogant coworker, or the quiet coworker bridges gaps, builds strength from diversity, and helps create an appreciative environment that's better for us all.

Applying Appreciative Environment

Ap-pre'ci-ate, v., 1. Valuing; the act of recognizing the best in people or the world around us; affirming past and present strengths, successes, and potentials; to perceive those things that give life to living systems. 2. To increase in value

En-vi'ron-ment, v., 1. A surrounding. 2. Conditions influencing development or growth.

Appreciative Environment begins with focusing on the value people around us possess and realizing that we have an effect on their opportunity to grow.

Gather your team together and ask the following questions to start. The application requires each of us to begin with understand ourselves better. Using the examples in this book, or your own, perform the following exercises.

Ask what you are especially good at doing.

- What do I move toward or have an interest in?
- How do I bring my best to the team and myself as an individual?
- Am I an introvert or extrovert, how does that work for me?
- When I am annoyed, what are my clues?

- How am I viewed by others?

Now repeat the questions focusing on a team member.

- What do they move toward or have an interest in?
- How do they bring their best to the team and themselves as an individual?
- Is my team member an introvert or extrovert, how does that work for them?
- When they are annoyed, what are their clues?
- How do they think they are viewed by others?

Have each team member discuss a positive about each team member.

Having an understanding of these basic questions will provide a great deal of insight into how you operate as an individual. Having an understanding of ourselves helps us in how we deal with others.

1. Re-frame organizational assessment.

- Look past one's own capability and accept that others have different levels of ability.

View the scenario, object, person, situation in a new light through critical thinking.

2. Focus on the follower's positive aspects.

- An employee who makes a mistake, is still a valuable asset. The individual who was a great employee does not become the worst based on a mistake. Focus on mistakes as a learning opportunity.

3. Focus on a positive path to improve followers' ability.

- Find the best in each employee, and learn to focus on those strengths. Once strengths are recognized areas to improve will be presented.

4. Embrace the individual and the diversification they bring to the organization.

- Encourage input from employees and welcome different opinions. Focus on the possible outcome of the sharing of knowledge. Focus on the positive future based on now and do not dwell on why past decisions are no longer valid.

Appreciative Environment indicates that the focus on the individual is just as important and that we should recognize and accept the individual for who they are. Focusing on the individual follower, and encouraging the diversity increases better ideas, innovation, and positive change activities. The outcome we strive for is less resistance to change and increase the transition from how work has been done to how the future needs work done.

An appreciative environment focuses on future and can help decrease the barriers to change. Once we have embraced the understanding of ourselves we can begin re-framing to build an Appreciative Environment.

Leaders should focus on the relationship with their fellow employees. Look for opportunities to highlight strengths and positives in order to create a genuine concern for the employee. Through relationship building and genuine concern the employees will increase their organizational commitment.

We should listen to each other's ideas, and show genuine interest. These steps will provide positive environments which increase followers' job satisfaction, increase employee commitment to the organization, and create a positive future.

The social significance is the ability of leadership to make better decisions with regard to how to drive followers' intrinsic motivation, autonomy, relatedness, and intention to quit. The Appreciative Environment provides opportunities to drive employees to grow in connecting and appreciation, creating successful organizations. The AE approach provides increased stimulating personal growth and learning and development opportunities as a pathway to more cohesive organizations.

Transparency

It is naive to believe or expect that each individual will get along personally. It is important to remember that no matter what is done there will be those who say, do, or perform in ways that cause friction. In my experience with creating an appreciative environment I have found it is okay and we should acknowledge that it is okay. Our goal is to help build strong professional teams.

During my years working in manufacturing the common make up of a team was a matrix format. Each member did not always work with each other and the Project Manager was not the main person over the technical members. Of course during the project, the team is expected to work as though they are a team.

On one particular project I had a couple of individuals who personally did not get along. Let's call them Andy and Bob, no that is not their real name. When I chose them for the project I was asked "why would you put Andy and Bob on the same team, you know they can't stand each other". My Program manager was concerned and thought I had set myself up for failure. The reason Andy & Bob were chosen was because they were each the best at what they did as technicians. I believed if we could get them to work on a professional level as a team, the short time frame we were provided could be met.

My first action was to sit down with the team, including Andy and Bob, and explain the project. The next thing I asked was for each person to explain what expertise they brought to the team and how they felt they could contribute to the project and the team.

During this team time the setting allowed me the opportunity to explain why each person was on the team and the reasons each could make the difference in success or failure of the project. We discussed one strength of each member and asked each person to share an area of difficulty. The difficulty was focused on something work related not personal. This provided an opportunity to share how we could each work together and help each other to achieve the main objective, the project.

Certainly the task was important and the reason for the team's existence, but building on the strength of each individual was important in order to build a stronger team. Building trust and respect and helping the team realize that we were all in the project together. The process allowed for increased buy in which we could benefit from in the long run.

Before ending the meeting, I explained that I expected us to work together. I encouraged the team to reach out for assistance from each other.

The conversation helped each team member increase their understanding of how together we could accomplish the end goal. I asked that if tension occurs for any reason let's not ignore it lets discuss it.

In ending the meeting, I reminded them this is not about us all being best buddies and hanging out at the bar together, this is about the project that together we can accomplish.

How did the project go? Glad you asked. Throughout the project Andy and Bob had occasion to butt heads, disagree, and at times need to take a break. Although most of the disagreements were productive and they were able to resolve the issues through open conversation and little assistance from the whole team. The weekly meetings became a great source to reinforce relationship building ideals and continue the focus on strengths, trust, and respect.

A key component was starting each meeting discussing the contributions and accomplishments we had as a team. By the end of the project Andy and Bob had learned to appreciate the work each did and built a level of trust at a professional level.

They never became social, although they found they could work together. Both of these men separately let me know they found a new respect for the other.

Due to the high performance of the team the project completed earlier than expected and under budget. This is a small sample of the power of creating an appreciative environment. It begins with the leader and being genuine, having open conversation, and empowering each to not have to be perfect and ask them to look for the strength in each other.

Remember the process is continuous and requires support and buy in. Do not force the process, it must grow organically over time. All of us have the power to create an appreciative environment. It is an ongoing often arduous task with a worthwhile objective toward creating high performing individuals and teams.

Research has shown leadership should embrace the Appreciative Environment philosophy as a method to create positive environments which can promote high productivity and effective organizations. Focusing on the future possibilities and accepting individuals input, positive change and adapting to the industry environment is possible.

Researchers like Hugo Munsterberg in 1913 believed that group association was not a definitive identity of the individual. Bertrand Russell, in 1949, questioned how best to recognize the individual and not hamper the individual creativity by forcing conformity to the group.

Other significance of this book is to provide you a positive focus on the individual and the positive work output which can come from appreciating each follower and coworker for the knowledge they bring to the organization. Situations are not always what they seem and each situation may be viewed differently due to our perceptions. Focus on strengths, build on those strengths to create opportunities and a positive future.

References

Allen, N. J., & Meyer, J. P. (1990). The measurement and antecedents of affective, continuance and normative commitment. *Journal of Occupational Psychology, 63,* 1-18.

N.A. (2002). *Leadership and self-deception.* Provo, UT: Arbinger Institute.

Austin, J. & Davies, S. (2000). Industrial and rganizational psychology: History of the field. *Encyclopedia of psychology, 4,* 252-255. (EBSCO host Accession Number: AN 2004-12702-108).

Bakker, A. B., Schaufeli, W. B., Leiter, M. P., & Taris, T. W. (2008). Work Engagement: An Emerging Concept. *Occupational Health Psychology. Work & Stress,* 22(3), 187- 200.

Bar-On, R. (2005). The bar-on model of emotional-social intelligence (ESI). *Issues in Emotional Intelligence,* 1(4): 1-28.

Binet, A. & Simon, T. (1916). *The development of*

intelligence in children. Baltimore, MD: Williams
& Wilkins Co.

Birknerová, Z. (2011). Social and Emotional Intelligence
in School Environment. *Asian Social Science,*
7(10), 241-248. doi:10.5539/ass.v7n10p241

Blake, A.M., & Moseley, J.L. (2011). Frederick Winslow
Taylor: One Hundred Years of Managerial Insight.
International Journal of Management, 28(4),
Part 2.

Bushe, G. R. (2012). Appreciative Inquiry: Theory and
Critique. In D. Boje, B. Burnes & J.
Hassard (Eds.), The Routledge Companion to
Organizational Change (pp. 87-103).
Oxford, UK: Routledge.

Blake, R.R., & Mouton, J.S. (1983). *Consultation: A
handbook for individual and organizational
development.* Reading, MA: Wesley-Addison.

Cameron, K.S. and Freeman, S.J. (1991), "Cultural

congruence, strength and type: Relationships
to effectiveness", in Woodman, R.W. and
Pasmore, W.A. (Eds), *Research in Organizational Change
and Development*, No. 5, JAI Press, Greenwich,
CT, pp. 23-58.

Cantor, N., & Kihlstrom, J.F. (1982). Cognitive and social
processes in personality. In G.T. Wilson & C.M.
Franks (Eds.), *Contemporary behavior therapy:
Conceptual and empirical foundations* (pp. 142-
201). New York, NY: Guilford.

Cantor, N., & Zirkel, S. (1990). Personality, cognition, and
purposive behavior. In L. Pervin(Ed.), *Handbook
of personality: Theory and research* (pp. 125-
164). New York, NY: Guilford.

Cherniss, C. (2000, April). *Emotional intelligence: What is
it and why it matters.* Paper presented at the

Annual Meeting of the Society for Industrial and Organizational Psychology. Retrieved from the Consortium for Research on Emotional Intelligence in Organizations Web site: www.eiconsortium.org

Cherniss, C., Goleman, D., Emmerling, R. J., Cowan, K., & Adler, M. (1998, October 7).

Bringing emotional intelligence to the workplace: A technical report issued by the consortium for research on emotional intelligence in organizations. New Brunswick, NJ: Consortium for Research on Emotional Intelligence in Organizations, Rutgers University. Retrieved from http://www.eiconsortium. org/reports/technical_report.html

Clawson, J.G. (2009). *Level three leadership: Getting below the surface (4 ed.).* Upper Saddle River, NJ: Pearson Prentice Hall.

Cooper, D.R. & Schindler, P.S. (2003). *Business research*

methods (8 ed). New York, NY: McGraw-Hill
Irwin.

Cooperrider, D.L. (1990). Positive Image, positive action:
The affirmative basis of organizing. In S.
Srivastva & D.L. Cooperrider (Eds.). *Appreciative*
Management and Leadership (91-125). San
Francisco, CA: Jossey-Bass.

Cooperrider, D. L., & Godwin, L. (2011). *Positive*
Organization Development: Innovation-
Inspired Change in an Economy and Ecology of
Strengths. In K. Cameron & G. Spreitzer (Eds.), The
Oxford Handbook of Positive Organizational
Scholarship (pp. 737 -750). New York: Oxford
University Press.

Cooperrider, D., Whitney, D., (2005). Appreciative
Inquiry: A Positive Revolution in
Change. San Francisco: Berrett-Koehler.

Cowardin-Lee, N., & Soyalp, N. (2011).

Improving organizational workflow with social network analysis and employee engagement constructs. *Consulting Psychology Journal: Practice and Research, 63*(4), 272-283. doi:10.1037/a0026754

Craig, J. B. (2008). *The relationship between the emotional intelligence of the principal and teacher job satisfaction.* (Order No. 3310476, University of Pennsylvania). *ProQuest Dissertations and Theses,* , 160-n/a. Retrieved from http://search.proquest.com/docview/304494361?accountid=35812. (prod. academic_MSTAR_304494361)

Creswell, J.W. (2009). *Research design: Qualitative, quantitative, and mixed methods approaches (3 ed.).* Thousand Oaks, CA: SAGE Publications, Inc.

Crowne, K. A. (2009). The relationships among social

intelligence, emotional intelligence and cultural

intelligence. *Organization Management Journal*,

6(3), 148-163.   doi:10.1057/omj.2009.20

Daft, R. (2005). The Leadership Experience, (3 ed).

Mason, Oh: Thomson Higher Education.

Dansereau, F., Graen, G., & Haga, W. J. (1975). A vertical

dyad approach to leadership within

formal organizations. *Organizational Behavior*

and Human Performance, 13, 46-78

Deming, E.W. (1982). *Out of crisis*. Cambridge, Mass:

MIT Center for Advanced Educational Services

Dixon, G. (2010). Emotions and Follower Behaviors in a

Time of Crisis. *SAE International.* Retrieved from

www.sae.org (Document ID: 2010-01-0681).

Drucker, P. F. (1999, Winter). Knowledge-worker

productivity: The biggest challenge.

California Management Review, 41(2), 79.

Fasihizadeh, Narjes; Oreyzi, Hamidreza; Nouri,

Aboulghasem. (2012). Investigation of positive affect and emotional intelligence effect on Job satisfaction among oil refinery personnel of Isfahan. Interdisciplinary Journal of Contemporary Research In Business 4.2 (Jun): 355-366.

Finkelstein, S., & Hambrick, D.C. (1996) *Strategic Leadership: Top Executives and their Effects On Organizations*. West, St. Paul, MN.

Fitzgerald, S. P., Murell, K. L., & Newman, H. L. (2002). Appreciative inquiry: The new frontier. In W. L. French, C. H. Bell, Jr., & R. A. Zawacki (Eds.), *Organizational development and transformation: Managing effective change* (6th ed.) (pp. 223-232). Boston: McGraw-Hill Irwin.

Gantt, H.L. (1919). *Organizing for work*. New York, NY: Harcourt, Brace and Howe, Inc.

Gardner, H. (1983). *Frames of mind: The theory of*

multiple intelligences. New York, NY: Basic Books.

Gardner, H. (1993). *Multiple intelligences: The theory in practice*. New York, NY: Basic Books.

Gardner, H. & Moran, S. (2006). The science of multiple intelligences theory: A response to Lynn Waterhouse. *Educational Psychologist*, 41(4): 227–232.

Goleman, D. (1995). EMOTIONAL INTELLIGENCE WHY IT CAN MATTER MORE THAN IQ. New York, NY: Bantam Books.

Goleman, D. (2006). Social Intelligence: THE NEW SCIENCE OF HUMAN RELATIONSHIPS. New York, NY: Bantam Books.

Greg, J. S., & Camilla, M. H. (2010). The joint influence of supervisor and subordinate emotional intelligence on leader-member exchange. *Journal of Business and Psychology,*

25(4), 593-605. doi:

http://dx.doi.org/10.1007/s10869-009-9152-y

Hackman, J.R., & Oldham, G.R. (1975). Development of
the job diagnostic survey. *Journal of
Applied Psychology,* 60 (2), 159-170.

Heinzman, J.R. (2005). Contingency Plans and Cultural
Management. *Business as a World
Business Conference.*

Heinzman, J.R., & Heinzman, J. (2004). Contingency
Plans and Cultural Management. *Clute
Management Journal & Conference.*

Hill, L.A. Where will we find tomorrow's leaders?
Harvard Business Review, (January, 2008), 123-139.

Hitt, M. A., & Tyler, B.B. (1991). 'Strategic decision
models: Integrating different
perspectives', *Strategic Management Journal*,
12(5), pp. 327–351.

Holman, P., Devane, T. & Cady, S. (2007). *The change handbook: The definitive resource on today's best methods for engaging whole systems,* 2nd Ed. San Francisco, CA: Berrett-Koehler.

Holmberg, L., & Reed, J. (2010). AI Research Notes. *AI Practitioner,* 12(4): 55-57.

Hsiao, Jui-Min; Chen, Yi-Chang (2012). ANTECEDENTS AND CONSEQUENCES OF JOB SATISFACTION: A CASE OF AUTOMOBILE COMPONENT MANUFACTURER IN TAIWAN. International Journal of Organizational Innovation (Online) 5.2 (Fall 2012): 164-178.

Hsi-An Shih, & Susanto, E. (2010). Conflict management styles, emotional intelligence, and job performance in public organizations. *International Journal of Conflict Management, 21*(2), 147-168. doi: http://dx.doi.org/10.1108/10444061011037387

Hunter, M. (2012). Creative intelligence and its

application to entrepreneurial opportunity and ethics.

Contemporary Readings in Law and Social Justice,

4(1), 69-149. Retrieved from

http://search.proquest.com/docview/1080807961?acc

ountid=35812

Ireland, R.D., Hitt, M.A., Bettis, R.A. and de Porres, D.A.

(1987); Strategy formulation processes:

Differences in perceptions of strengths and

weaknesses indicators and environmental

uncertainty by managerial level. *Strategic*

Management Journal, Sept - Oct 1987, 8(5).

pp. 469-486.

Katz, R.L. (1955). Skills of an Effective Administrator.

Harvard Business Review, 33(1): 33-42.

Kobe, L.M., Reiter-Palmon, R., & Rickers, J.D. (2001). Self-reported leadership experiences in relation to inventoried social and emotional intelligence. *Current Psychology: Developmental, Learning, Personality, Social,* 20(2): 154-163.

Kiesler, S., & Sproull, L. (1982). 'Managerial response to changing environments: Perspectives on problem sensing from social cognition', *Administrative Science Quarterly,* **27**, pp. 548–570.

Kreitner, R., & Kinicki, A. (2013). *Organizational behavior (10th e.d.).* New York, NY: McGraw-Hill Irwin.

Lawler, G.E., & Worley, C.G. (2011). *Management reset: organizing for sustainable effectiveness.* San Francisco, CA: Jossey-Bass.

Leiter, M. P., Day, A., Oore, D., & Spence Laschinger, H. K. (2012). Getting better and staying better: Assessing civility, incivility, distress, and job attitudes one year after a civility intervention.

Journal Of Occupational Health Psychology,
17(4), 425-434. doi:10.1037/a0029540

Lowe, D., Levitt, K.J., and Wilson, T. (2008). Solutions
for retaining generation Y followers in the
workforce. *Business Renaissance Quarterly*, Fall
2008, 3(3), 43-57.

Lund, D.B. (2003). Organizational culture and job
satisfaction. *Journal of Business & Industrial
Marketing.* 18(3), 219-236.

Mann, C.R. (1918). *A study of engineering education.*
Boston, MA: The Merrymount Press.

Marlowe, H.A. (1986). Social intelligence: Evidence for
multidimensionality and construct
independence. *Journal of Educational Psychology*,
78(1): 52–58.

Marlowe, H.A., & Bedell, J.R. (1982). Social Intelligence:
Evidence for independence of the construct.
Psychology Reports, 51, 461-462.

McNeilly, M.R.(2012). *Sun Tzu and the art of business:*

six strategic principles for managers.

New York, NY: Oxford University Press.

Meyer, J.P., Allen, N.J., & Smith, C.A. (1993).

Commitment to organizations and occupations:

Extension and test of a three-component

conceptualization. *Journal of Applied*

Psychology, 78(4), 538-551.

Miller, K. (2005). Organizational Culture and the Bottom

Line Case Study. *SME Technical Papers*

Database. Retrieved from www.sme.org.

(Document ID: TP05PUB210).

Mirchandani, D., Ikerd, J. (2008). Building and

maintaining sustainable organizations.

Organization Management Journal, 5, 40-51.

Mischel, W., (1973). Toward a cognitive social learning

reconceptualization of personality.

Psychological Review, 80, 252-28.

Mohrman, S., (2006). Having Relevance and Impact. *The*

Journal of Applied Behavioral Science, 36 43, 12-22.

Montgomery, C.A. Putting leadership back into strategy.

    Harvard Business Review, (January, 2008), 54-60.

Munsterberg, H. (1913). *Psychology and industrial*

    efficiency. Boston, MA: Houghton Mifflin

    Company.

Nonaka, I., & Nishiguchi, T. (2001). *Knowledge*

    emergence social, technical, and evolutionary

    dimensions of knowledge creation. New York,

    NY: Oxford University Press, Inc.

Porter, M.E. The five competitive forces that shape

    strategy. *Harvard Business Review,* (January,

    2008), 78-93.

Robbins, S.P. (2003). *Organizational behavior: concepts,*

    controversies, and applications (7th

    ed.). Upper Saddle River, NJ: Prentice-Hall.

Robbins, S.P., & Judge, T.A. (2012). *The essentials of*

    organizational behavior (15 ed.). Upper Saddle

River, NJ: Prentice Hall.

Rogelberg, S.G. (2007). *Encyclopedia of Industrial and Organizational Psychology,* University of North Carolina Charlotte, Sage Publications, Inc.

Royal, C.L. (2006). Organizational Development and Appreciative Inquiry; A Transformative Next Step for Social Justice and Diversity Practitioners. *NTL Organizational Development Handbook.*

Russell, B. (1949). *Authority and the individual.* Boston, MA: Beacon Press.

Salovey, P. & Mayer, J.D. (1990). Emotional Intelligence. *Imagination, Cognition & Personality,* 9(3): 185-211.

Sariolghalam, N., Noruzi, M.R., & Rahimi, G.R. (2010). The Enigma of Howard Gardner's Multiple Intelligences Theory in the Area of Organizational Effectiveness. *International Journal of Business and Management,* 5(5), 161-171.

Schmidt, F.L., Hunter, J. (2004). General Mental Ability in the World of Work: Occupational Attainment and Job Performance. *Journal of Personality and Social Psychology.* 86(1), 162-173.

Senge, P.M. (1996). Leading Learning Organizations. *Training & Development.* December, 36-37.

Shih, H., Susanto, E. (2010). Conflict Management styles, emotional intelligence, and job performance in public organ izational. *International Journal of conflict management*, 21 (2), 147 – 168.

Siegel, L.M. (2008). *The effects of appreciative inquiry on emotional intelligence.* Ashland, OH: Ashland University.

Snyder, M., & Cantor, N. (1998). Understanding personality and social behavior: A functionalist strategy. In D.T. Gilbert & S.T. Fiske (Eds.), *Handbook of social psychology*, 4th ed. (Vol. 2, pp. 635-679). Boston, MA: McGraw-Hill.

Sonnenfeld, J. (1983). Academic learning, worker
    learning, and the Hawthorne studies, *Social
    Forces,* 61, 904-909.

Sternberg, R.J. (1997). Managerial intelligence: why IQ
    isn't enough. JOURNAL OF MANAGEMENT,
    23, 475-493.

Sternberg, R.J. (1985). Beyond IQ: a triarchic theory of
    human intelligence. New York, NY:
    Cambridge University Press.

Su-Chao, C., & Ming-Shing, L. (2007). A study on
    relationship among leadership, organizational
    culture, the operation of learning organization and
    employees' job satisfaction. *The Learning
    Organization, 14*(2), 155-185. ID:
    10.1108/09696470710727014

Taylor, F.W. (1911). *The principles of scientific
    management.* New York, NY: Harper & Brothers
    Publishers.

Thatchenkery, T. (2005). *Appreciative sharing of knowledge, leveraging knowledge management for strategic change*. Chagrin Falls, OH: Taos Institute Publications.

Thatchenkery, T. & Metzker, C. (2006). *Appreciative Intelligence*, San Francisco, CA: Barrett- Koehler Publishing House.

The Score Code of Ethics and Conduct. (2013). Retrieved from www.score.org.

Thorndike, E.L. (1920). Intelligence and its use. Harper's Magazine, 140, 227-235.

Thorndike, E.L. (1913). Theory of mental and social measurements (2 e.d.). New York, NY: Columbia University.

Tsai, Y. (2011). Relationship between Organizational Culture, Leadership Behavior and Job Satisfaction. *BMC Health Services Research.* 11:98.

Tucker, J. S., Sinclair, R. R., Mohr, C. D., Adler, A. B.,

Thomas, J. L., & Salvi, A. D. (2009). Stress and counterproductive work behavior: Multiple relationships between demands, control, and soldier indiscipline over time. *Journal Of Occupational Health Psychology*, *14*(3), 257-271. doi:10.1037/a0014951

Verleysen, B., & Van Acker, F. (2012). Appreciative Inquiry Evaluated from a Self-Deterministic Perspective: The Impact on Psychological Capital. Retrieved from www.2012WAIC.com.

Wagner, R.K., & Sternberg, R.J. (1985). Practical intelligence in real-world pursuits: The roles of tacit knowledge. *Journal of Personality & Social Psychology*, 49, 436-458.

Weller, D.L. (1999). Application of the multiple intelligences theory in quality organizations. *Team Performance Management,* 5(4), 136-146.